LITTLE JOURNEYS WITH JESUS

60 Devotions and Activities with Small Children

Jeanette L. Groth

Illustrated by Joanne Goin

Publishing House
St. Louis

Copyright © 1984 Concordia Publishing House
3558 South Jefferson Avenue
St. Louis, Missouri 63118
Printed in the United States of America

All rights reserved. No part of this publication may be reproduced, stored in a retrieval system, or transmitted, in any form or by any means, electronic, mechanical, photocopying, recording, or otherwise, without the prior written permission of Concordia Publishing House.

Library of Congress Cataloging in Publication Data

Groth, Jeanette L., 1947-
    Little journeys with Jesus.

    Summary: The reader is led on a devotional journey stopping at 60 places in the life and ministry of Jesus Christ from His birth to His ascension. Each stop is marked with a reading, discussion questions, and a prayer.
    1. Children — Prayer-books and devotions — English. 2. Jesus Christ — Prayer-books and devotions — English. [1. Jesus Christ — Prayer-books and devotions. 2. Prayer-books and devotions] I. Title.
BV4870.G78 1984   242'.62   83-18825
ISBN 0-570-03924-X

3 4 5 6 7 8 9 10   93 92 91 90 89 88

The Epistle of James emphasizes faith in action. This book is dedicated to James Lawrence Gagan Sr., whose kindnesses and love for children have shown our family "faith in action."

INTRODUCTION

Going on a vacation or field trip may produce countless learning opportunities. Many of the "journeys" may also bring pleasant experiences with family and friends that are never forgotten. In this devotional booklet you are asked to take a journey with Jesus. Through this journey you will go to many places He traveled in His ministry here on earth. You will also be studying along the way. As you read His Word, do the activities and pray that you will grow closer to Jesus and to each other. Have a good journey!

CONTENTS

A Trip to Bethlehem	8
Some Early Visitors	10
To a Faraway Land	12
A Holiday Trip	14
When Mary and Joseph Could Not Find Jesus	16
To the Jordan River	18
When Jesus Was Tempted	20
To a Wedding	22
To the Temple	24
A Chat with Nicodemus	26
To a Well	28
A Catch of Fish	30
To Pick Some Disciples	32
To Simon Peter's House	34
A Talk with the Heavenly Father	36
A Hillside Sermon	38
To Heal a Servant	40
To Talk to John the Baptist's Followers	42
To a Stormy Lake	44
To Visit a Sick Girl	46
To Feed a Hungry Crowd	48
A Story About Neighbors	50
A Meeting on the Water	52
To a Friend's for Supper	54
A Meal at Simon's House	56
To Help a Poor Widow	58
An Eye-opening Experience	60
To Heal 10 Men	62
To Sit on Jesus' Lap	64
To a Place Above a City	66
To Visit Sad Friends	68
To a Poolside	70

To a Fig Tree	72
To Visit a Tree Climber	74
To Jesus' Home	76
A Talk with a Rich Young Man	78
A Poor Woman's Offering	80
To Open Ears	82
A Lesson on Prayer	84
A Mountain Vision	86
Sending Out the Disciples	88
A Look at the Future	90
In a Parade	92
To a Special Supper	94
To a Foot Washing	96
To a Garden to Pray	98
A Garden Meeting	100
To the High Priest's Court	102
At a Fireside	104
To Another Trial	106
The Soldiers' Mean Game	108
On a Hard Walk	110
At the Cross	112
To See Jesus Die	114
To the Tomb of Jesus	116
In the Tomb's Garden	118
On the Emmaus Road	120
In a Closed Room	122
To a Seashore Breakfast	124
To a Hillside Gathering	126

A TRIP TO BETHLEHEM

Luke 2:1-7

We will start our travels with Jesus by going where His life on earth began. We will visit the little town of Bethlehem. Jesus was born in Bethlehem. At the time of Jesus' birth the Romans ruled the country where Mary and Joseph lived. The Roman ruler decided to count all the people by sending them back to the towns their families came from. He wanted to do this so that he could charge them money to run the Roman government. Since Mary and Joseph were from David's family, they had to return to David's home town, Bethlehem.

The town of Bethlehem was crowded. Mary and Joseph could not find a place to stay. Finally, an innkeeper let them use his stable. There by the animals Jesus, our Savior, was born.

As God, Jesus lived in His beautiful home in heaven. Because He loved us, He left that home, became a baby, and came to earth to live. Since all people are sinners, Jesus was born to live, suffer, and die on the cross. His death would give all people forgiveness for their sins. That is why Jesus came to earth.

PRAYER IDEA
Thank Jesus for coming to earth to die for you.

QUESTIONS
1. Where was Jesus born?
2. What does it mean when we say Jesus came to earth?
3. Why are you glad that Jesus was born?

ACTIVITIES

a. Using cardboard, make the outline of a simple cross. Punch a hole in the top so it can be hung. Decorate it with paints, markers, or crayons. You might also glue on beads, sequins, or macaroni to make it an attractive ornament. Hang it up. Then put the cross with your Christmas ornaments to remind you why Jesus was born on earth.

b. Have a Christmas carol song time. Which Christmas songs remind you of the reason Jesus was born?

c. Have your parents show you a Bible map. They will point out to you the town of Bethlehem where Jesus was born. You might want to look at picture books, Christmas cards, etc., to find ideas of how the town of Bethlehem might have looked at Jesus' time.

MATERIALS

cardboard for cross
materials to decorate cross
    (markers, paints, crayons,
    beads, sequins, macaroni)
glue
map showing Bethlehem
pictures of Bethlehem in
    Jesus' day

SOME EARLY VISITORS

Luke 2:8-20

Usually when a new baby is born, people wait for a while to visit. They let the new mother and baby get settled in. But on the very night He was born, Mary, Joseph, and Baby Jesus had some excited visitors. Shepherds had been taking care of their sheep out on a hillside. Suddenly an angel came to them and told them that their Savior was born in Bethlehem. Then many, many angels came to sing praises to God for the birth of this special baby.

After the angels left, the shepherds began talking to each other. "Let's go to Bethlehem," they said. "Let's see this wonderful baby."

So they hurried to Bethlehem. There in the stable they saw the newborn baby. They knew that He was the promised Savior. They got down on their knees and praised and thanked God for this wonderful child.

Soon they left and started back to their fields. Their hearts were so full of joy. They wanted everyone to know their good news. They stopped people and told them about the newborn Savior.

PRAYER IDEA
Thank God for the Good News about Jesus.

QUESTIONS
1. What was the Good News the shepherds heard?
2. Who told them this Good News?
3. What did they do when they heard this Good News?

ACTIVITIES
a. Get a large sheet of paper. Across the top put the words "GOOD NEWS." Beneath these large words put "The Savior, Jesus, is born." You might decorate this page with a picture of Jesus and His family in the stable.

b. Cut an oatmeal box in half. Cover it with brown paper. Glue some cardboard half-circles on it for legs. You might fill this manger with straw or strips of yellow paper. Put a small doll in it. Use this to remind you that Jesus, the Savior, was born for you.

c. Take an 11" x 17" piece of construction paper. Use old Christmas cards. Cut out pictures of the shepherds and the newborn baby. Glue these pictures onto the construction paper. Cover the whole thing with clear adhesive vinyl. You might give this place mat to a friend to share with them the Good News that Jesus is born.

MATERIALS
large piece of paper
crayons
oatmeal box
yellow and brown
    construction paper
cardboard
glue
scissors
11" x 17" construction paper
old Christmas cards
clear adhesive vinyl

TO A FARAWAY LAND

Matthew 2:13-23

Sometimes the trips people take are not very happy. Sometimes they have to travel fast in order to keep themselves and their families safe. When Jesus was still very small, His family had to take a trip like that, too.

Wise Men had come to visit the baby Jesus. They bowed down and worshiped Him. They even brought Him presents of gold and sweet perfume and spices.

After the men leave, Joseph lies down to sleep. While he is sleeping, he has an important dream. In this dream God tells him to take little Jesus to Egypt. King Herod has heard about Jesus and is worried that He is going to be a king. He decides to kill all babies in and around Bethlehem so that he will get rid of this Jesus. God says that Joseph must hurry and take Jesus away so that He will be safe. So Mary, Joseph, and Jesus quickly leave for far-off Egypt.

God took care of His Son, Jesus. He takes care of us in many wonderful ways today.

PRAYER IDEA
Ask God to keep you safe always.

QUESTIONS
1. Who told Jesus to leave Bethlehem?
2. Why was this trip important?
3. What are some ways God keeps us safe today?

ACTIVITIES
a. What does it mean to say we have guardian angels?

b. Use pipe cleaners and twist them into a simple angel outline. Hang this angel in your room to remind you that God's angels are watching over you to keep you safe.

c. Use old magazines. Cut out as many arms of different people as you can find. Glue them onto a piece of paper. Over them write, "Underneath are His everlasting arms." Talk about how God is always there to keep you safe and do what is best for you.

MATERIALS
pipe cleaners
old magazines
glue
large sheets of paper or posterboard
crayons or markers

A HOLIDAY TRIP

Luke 2:41-42

A special trip is always a treat. It's always fun to go to a circus, a show, or on a shopping adventure. Come along with Jesus as He takes a special holiday trip to the temple.

Jesus is 12 years old, and His family is going to spend the Passover holiday in Jerusalem. This day is special because it is a reminder to the people that God had brought them safely out of Egypt many years before. Each year God's people have a special celebration to think about God's goodness and love for them. How wonderful to worship with family and friends in the temple in Jerusalem!

Even the trip to Jerusalem is an adventure. Walking along and chatting with family and friends is always fun. Perhaps camping at night and singing and eating together reminded Jesus of how wonderful it is to be a part of God's family. What a treat to go to the Passover in Jerusalem!

It is wonderful for us to be a part of God's family. It is special for us to worship and work together.

PRAYER IDEA
Thank God that you are part of His family.

QUESTIONS
1. Where was Jesus going? Why?
2. What was the Passover?

ACTIVITIES
a. Draw a picture of a place you have visited with your family. What was fun about going there?

b. Sing a favorite Jesus song together. Why is it good to have Jesus as part of your family?

c. Can you remember going to a special holiday church service? What made it special for you?

MATERIALS
paper   crayons or markers

WHEN MARY AND JOSEPH COULD NOT FIND JESUS

Luke 2:43-52

In a large store it is often easy to wander away from your parents. Then parents need to spend time looking for you. If there is a toy department, they may know exactly where to find you.

The Passover celebration was over. The villagers were returning to their homes. Large groups of people were walking, talking, singing, and enjoying the happiness of time together. Soon it was time to stop and set up camp for the night. Mary and Joseph said to each other, "Have you seen Jesus?" Each answered, "I thought He was with you." Then they began asking their friends and family if they had seen Him.

Quickly Mary and Joseph ran back to Jerusalem. Where was Jesus? They found Him in the temple talking with the church teachers and leaders. How surprised these men were at how much Jesus knew about God's Word!

Then Jesus' mother said, "Didn't You know You worried us?"

Jesus answered, "Didn't you know I would be in My Father's house?" Then He went home to Nazareth to grow and learn.

PRAYER IDEA
Ask God to help you learn more about His Word.

QUESTIONS
1. Why would Jesus know so much about God's Word?
2. Why were the teachers and leaders surprised that Jesus knew so much?
3. Why did Jesus call the temple His Father's house?

ACTIVITIES
a. Have each person in your family tell their favorite Bible verse or Bible story. (Perhaps younger children can do this by sharing a picture in an Arch Book or Bible story book.)

b. God's Word was written on a scroll in Jesus' day. Use two sticks and attach them to a long strip of paper. Print a simple Bible verse on the paper. Roll it from each end to make your own Bible scroll.

c. Look in Bible story books and find a picture of Jesus' temple church. Use your blocks to build a church. Talk about the things God's people do together in church.

MATERIALS
sticks
paper
glue

Bible story book with a temple picture
blocks

TO THE JORDAN RIVER

Matthew 3:13-17

John the Baptist had been preaching and telling people to change. "The Savior is coming!" he said. "Leave your sinful ways! Quit doing what is bad!" Come along with Jesus on a visit with John at the Jordan River.

When Jesus and His followers got to the Jordan River, Jesus wanted John to baptize Him. But John said, "Why do You come to me? You are greater than I am. I ought to be baptized by You. I'm not even good enough to tie Your shoes." Finally John did as Jesus asked and baptized Him.

How surprised the crowd must have been! When Jesus was baptized, the heavens opened, and the Spirit of God came down like a dove. God the Father's voice called from heaven and said, "This is my Son, whom I love. I am happy with Him."

Jesus was God, but He was also a person who was doing all the things that make God happy. Jesus also helps us to know what pleases God as we study and learn His Word.

PRAYER IDEA

Thank God for your baptism. Ask Him to help you to do things that please Him.

QUESTIONS
1. Who was John the Baptist?
2. What was his job?
3. Why was Jesus baptized?

ACTIVITIES
a. Ask your parents to show you your own baptismal certificate. When is your baptismal birthday? What happened at your Baptism?

b. God was pleased with His Son, Jesus. God is pleased with us when we do loving and kind things. Make gift coupons of loving things you can do for family members, like picking up toys, setting the table, taking out the garbage. Give them these coupons as an I-love-you gift.

c. Decorate a candle with acrylic paints, felt scraps, or sequins. Light it to celebrate each time someone in your family or class has a baptismal birthday.

MATERIALS
paper
candle
glue

felt scraps, sequins, or acrylic paint

WHEN JESUS WAS TEMPTED

Matthew 4:1-11

Did you ever want to be alone? Maybe you just wanted to spend some moments thinking.

Jesus wanted to be alone, so He went out to the desert. While He was there, the devil came to tempt Him. Jesus had not been eating, so He was hungry. The devil tempted Him by saying, "If you are the Son of God, turn these stones to bread."

But Jesus said, "Man does not live by bread only, but also by God's Word." Jesus knew that God's Word and will would tell Him not to follow the tempting of the devil.

Next the devil wanted Jesus to jump from a high place on the temple to prove He was God's son. But Jesus knew He was God's Son, and He reminded the Devil that he should not tempt God.

Then the devil told Jesus that the whole world would be His if He would just bow down to worship him. Jesus quickly told Satan to get away. "Don't you know that God's Word says that you should only worship Him?" said Jesus.

Then the devil left Jesus. Jesus had proved that He was strong enough not to listen to the devil. God's Word can give us this strength.

PRAYER IDEA
Ask God to help you to do what is right.

QUESTIONS
1. How did Jesus know that God would not want Him to do what the devil tried to get Him to do?
2. How does the devil tempt us?
3. What can we do when the devil tries to get us to do bad things?

ACTIVITIES
a. Use old magazines. Cut out pictures of people doing things that please God. Put these on one half of a large sheet of paper. Then cut out pictures of people who are pleasing the devil and glue them on the other half. You might title your poster, "Whom will you serve?" As you work, talk about times when you have followed Jesus and other times when you have followed the devil's tempting.

b. God's Word always turns the devil away. Learn the Bible verse, "The Lord will rescue me from every evil" (2 Timothy 4:18). Say it when you feel tempted so you will remember Jesus' power for your life.

c. Make puppets out of paper bags. Act out times in your life when you have been tempted or may be tempted to do something bad. As a family, discuss what you could do to please Jesus in each situation.

MATERIALS
large sheets of paper or
    posterboard
glue
magazines and newspapers
markers or crayons

paper lunch bags
fabric or construction paper
    scraps
yarn scraps

TO A WEDDING

John 2:1-11

A party, a party! All of us like parties. We like to be with our friends. We like to have a good time and enjoy good things to eat. Come along with Jesus to a wedding party.

Jesus went to this party with His mother, His brothers, and His disciple followers. While they were there enjoying the party, a sad thing happened—they ran out of wine. Jesus saw six big stone jars standing near Him. He asked some of the workers to fill the jars with water. They filled them to the top. Then Jesus told them to take some out of the jars to the head of the party. The head of the party tasted the liquid from the jars. How surprised everyone was when he said that this was the best wine of all!

Jesus had done a miracle. Jesus had helped His friends. He had shown His power over things. His disciples believed that He was God. Jesus helps us and shows us that He cares about the things that happen to us every day.

PRAYER IDEA

Thank Jesus for caring about your everyday problems and helping with them.

QUESTIONS
1. How did Jesus help at this wedding party?
2. What do we call what Jesus did?
3. Why do you think Jesus did miracles?

ACTIVITIES

a. Using clay or playdough, mold some jars to remind you of a time Jesus showed His power. (Playdough Recipe: To 2 cups boiling water add 3 tablespoons salad oil plus food coloring. Add 2½ cups flour, ½ cup salt, and 1 tablespoon powdered alum. Knead well. Store in a sealed plastic container.)

b. Act out the Bible story for today.

c. Make a list of the ways Jesus shows He cares about us (clothing, food, home, etc., but most of all His death and resurrection for us).

MATERIALS
clay or playdough
    For playdough recipe:
water
salad oil
food coloring
flour
salt
alum

TO THE TEMPLE

John 2:13-16

What are some things you do when you go to church? You probably said, "Sing, pray, and hear God's Word." Come along with Jesus and His followers to His temple church. They also went to their temple to pray and hear God's Word. When they got there, Jesus was very angry with what He saw. Instead of a place to pray and hear God's Word, it was more like a store. Some people were selling animals for the sacrifices. Some people were exchanging money for people from faraway lands. There was loud shouting for people to "Come and buy!"

Jesus upset the sellers' tables. He chased away the animals that people were selling. Then He said, "My Father's house is to be a place to pray, not a place for selling."

We too can go to God's house to worship and praise God for the wonderful things He has done for us. Here we can learn more about Jesus. We can learn new ways to show our thanks and love for Him.

PRAYER IDEA
Ask God to help you worship Him in your church.

QUESTIONS
1. Why was Jesus angry?
2. What is God's house to be used for?
3. What is your favorite part of the church service? Why?

ACTIVITIES
a. Do the finger play "Here is the church. Here is the steeple. Open the doors, and see all the people." Talk about the things God's people do in their church home.

b. Sing "The Church Bell," arranged by J. C. Wohlfeil, from *Little Children, Sing to God!* (Concordia Publishing House, 1960):

> Dingdong, dingdong,
>   church bells ring.
> Come to church
>   to pray and sing.

c. Use blocks or clay to make a simple model of your church building.

MATERIALS
Little Children, Sing to God!   blocks or clay

A CHAT WITH NICODEMUS

John 3:1-21

A baby that is just born is new to everything. It has so much to learn and so much growing to do. Come along with Jesus to an evening chat with a ruler named Nicodemus.

Nicodemus told Jesus that he knew He was a teacher from God. He said that he could tell this by the way Jesus taught and the things He did. Jesus said that he was right. He also said that to be a part of God's family it was important to be born again.

Nicodemus was surprised. He knew that he could not be a tiny newborn baby again. Then Jesus told him that he could be born again by being baptized. Then he would have a new life. He would be a child of God. God would make him a new person who would have much growing and learning to do.

We too are part of God's family. When we believe in Jesus and are baptized, the Holy Spirit will also help us know and do many things that make Jesus happy. We can have fun as we grow in Jesus each day.

PRAYER IDEA
Thank God for your rebirth.

QUESTIONS
1. Why do you think Nicodemus came to Jesus at night?
2. What did Jesus say was important in order to be part of God's family?
3. How is Baptism like a birth?

ACTIVITIES
a. Make a list of the many things a baby will need to learn as it grows to be an adult. How can God be a part of a baby's learning?

b. Make a collage out of baby pictures from magazines or your own family. Over the pictures put "New Life." In the center of the poster write your family's baptismal dates. Talk about the time you were reborn through Baptism.

c. Use fabric and fabric crayons to make a special baby book for a baby friend of yours. Pink the edges of some washable materials. Old sheets work well. Draw some simple pictures, and set the crayon with an iron. Sew the pages together.

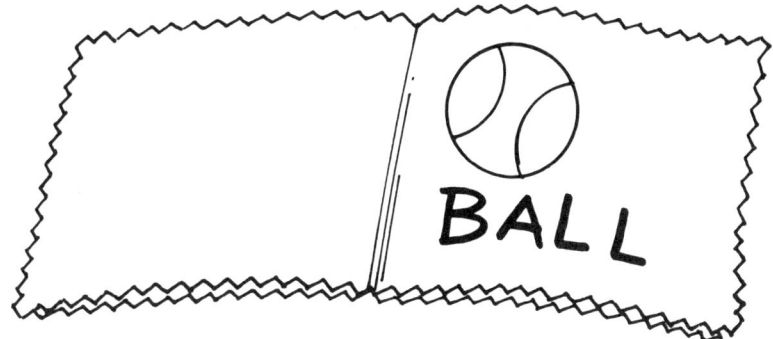

MATERIALS
magazines
glue
paper or posterboard

washable material
pinking scissors
fabric crayons or paints

TO A WELL

John 4:4-30

Think of a time when you came in from playing and were hot and thirsty. How good a cool glass of water tasted!

Come with Jesus to a well. As Jesus arrives tired and thirsty, He sees a woman from another country. He asks this woman for a drink. Usually people from Jesus' country and people from this woman's country did not get along, so the woman was surprised that Jesus even asked her this favor.

The woman asked, "How is it that you ask me for a drink?"

Jesus said, "The water I would give you would keep you from ever being thirsty again." Then the woman asked Jesus for this water. Jesus told her many things about her life. He also told her that He was the promised Savior. Her thirst for forgiveness and a Savior were filled.

Jesus takes care of all our needs. He gives us forgiveness and a home in heaven.

PRAYER IDEA
Ask Jesus to be your Living Water.

QUESTIONS

1. Why was the woman surprised that Jesus asked her for a drink?

2. What did Jesus have to share with this woman?

3. How did Jesus give the woman what she needed most?

ACTIVITIES

a. Use a can as your well. Tie a screw-on cap to a string. Show how the woman would need to lower a jar into the well to get water.

b. Make a list of the many ways we use water. You might cut out pictures to show this. Water is a basic need for life. Jesus, the Living Water, is needed for life eternal.

c. Make a sign and put it by your water faucet: "Jesus, the Living Water." Let it remind you that Jesus takes care of our needs.

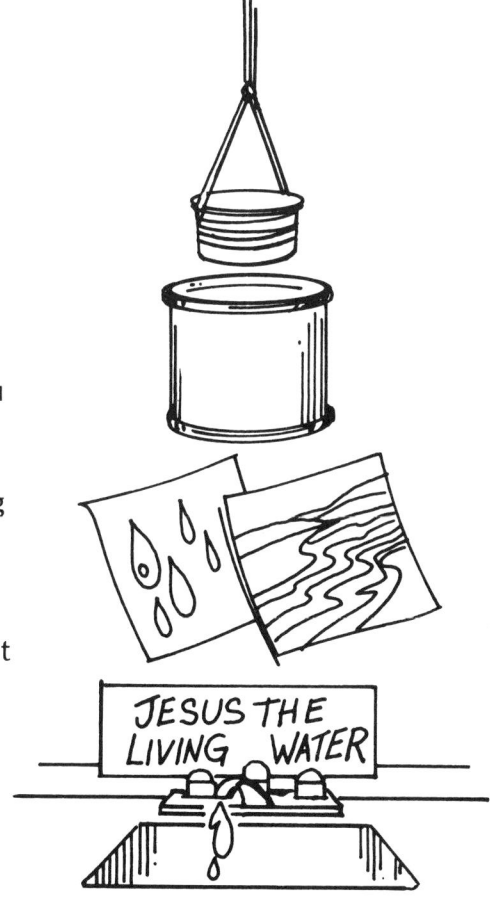

MATERIALS

can
screw-on cap
string
cardboard or construction paper
crayons or markers

A CATCH OF FISH

Luke 5:1-9

Have you ever gone fishing? If you have, perhaps you have sat for a long time and caught nothing at all. Come along with Jesus as He shares God's Word by a lake.

As Jesus was talking, people kept getting closer and closer to Him. Finally He saw two boats by the lake. The men who had been fishing in them were washing their nets. Jesus asked one of them if He could preach from his boat. Then He taught the people. When He finished, He said to Simon, who owned the boat, "Put out your nets to catch some fish."

Simon said, "Jesus, we fished all night, but we did not catch anything. But because You tell me to, I will put out the nets."

Soon the nets were out. At once they were so full of fish that they began to break. Simon called for his partners in another boat to come and help him take in the catch. There were so many fish that both boats began to sink.

At once Simon Peter knew how great Jesus was. He knew that Jesus was his Lord and his God. Jesus our Lord does great things for us.

PRAYER IDEA
Thank God for His greatness to you.

QUESTIONS

1. Where was Jesus preaching?
2. How did He show His greatness?
3. In what ways does Jesus show His greatness to you?

ACTIVITIES

a. Fold a paper in half. Cut out a simple fish shape. On the fish write, "God is great." You might use each person's fish and make a mobile for your family.

b. Take turns in your family telling why you think that Jesus is great.

c. Use the prayer "God is great. God is good. Let us thank Him for our food. Amen."

MATERIALS

paper
scissors

string or thread and hanger (optional)

TO PICK SOME DISCIPLES

Luke 5:8-11

Play a little of the game follow-the-leader. Do you see that when one person does an action, everyone else copies that action? Come along as Jesus is the Leader.

He has just shown Peter, James, and John how great He is by doing a miracle. When these men put out their nets, they caught many fish. They were afraid because they saw Jesus' great power. But Jesus said, "Don't be afraid. I want you to be My followers. I want you to catch men." Jesus wanted these men to learn many things from Him. He wanted them to tell others of His greatness. He wanted them to make other people His followers, too.

Peter, James, and John did not stop for a minute. They were anxious to follow their new Leader. They left everything—boats, fish, family, and friends—to follow Jesus.

Jesus wants us to follow Him. He wants us to share the news that He is the Savior with others. He wants us to help Him find more followers today.

PRAYER IDEA

Ask Jesus to help you follow Him and lead others to know Him.

QUESTIONS
1. Whom did Jesus pick to follow Him?
2. Can you name some other men who followed Jesus?
3. What did Jesus want these men to learn by following Him?

ACTIVITIES
a. Use a pipe cleaner. Bend it into a hook shape. Twist a loop on the top so you can wear the fish hook. Wear it and see if you can tell someone else about being a fisher for Jesus.

b. As a family, make an invitation to someone that you know who does not have a church.

c. Play another game of follow-the-leader. Talk about some ways you can follow your Leader, Jesus.

MATERIALS
pipe cleaners   paper
string or yarn   crayons or markers

TO SIMON PETER'S HOUSE

Matthew 8:14-17

It's always fun to visit a friend's home. Come along with Jesus as He is visiting at the home of His friend Simon Peter.

As Jesus arrives at Peter's home, everyone is not happy and well. Peter's mother-in-law is sick with a high fever. Peter and his family are probably a bit worried about her.

Quickly Jesus shows this family His love for them. He puts His hand on the sick woman. At once her fever is gone. In fact she feels so good that she gets up and is ready to fix food and serve Jesus. How grateful this family must have felt for Jesus' care and love!

Soon many others come to Peter's home to have Jesus heal them. Jesus does this lovingly, too. He cares about others. As one writer of God's Word says, "He took our hurts and healed our sickness." Most of all He takes away the hurt of our sin and gives us heaven as our home. That is the greatest act of love.

PRAYER IDEA
Ask God to bless doctors, nurses, and friends who care for people who are ill.

QUESTIONS

1. Whom was Jesus visiting?
2. Why was there some unhappiness in this family?
3. How did Jesus show that He cared for this family?

ACTIVITIES

a. Make a list of people you know who are ill. Use this as a family prayer list, and pray for them each day. Be sure to thank God when they are well.

b. Learn this prayer to say when you are ill:

Tender Jesus, meek and mild,
Look upon a little child.
Help me, if it is your will,
To recover from all ill.

c. Make a get-well card. Fold paper to make a card. Decorate the outside with scraps of felt, crayons, or cutout pictures. Inside write a simple message like "God cares for you." Send it to someone you know who is ill.

MATERIALS

paper
crayons or markers
felt
old magazines
glue

A TALK WITH THE HEAVENLY FATHER

Mark 1:35-39

When do you pray to Jesus? Maybe you pray before and after meals. Maybe you talk to Jesus before you go to bed. Perhaps you talk to Him when you have a special problem during the day. Come along with Jesus as He talks to His heavenly Father.

Jesus had been busy making people well. He wanted to show people that He loved and cared for them. He wanted to show them His power as God. It had been a busy day. Jesus was tired, so He lay down to sleep. Then He got up early and went out by Himself. He spent time alone talking to His heavenly Father in prayer. Soon His disciples came looking for Him. Jesus reminded them that He must travel to many other places so that many more people would come to know Him.

We also need to take time out of our busy days to talk with Jesus. We can learn about Him from God's Word. We can talk with Him when we pray.

PRAYER IDEA
Ask God to keep you close and talking to Him in prayer.

QUESTIONS
1. Why was Jesus tired?
2. How did Jesus talk to His heavenly Father?
3. Why did Jesus travel to many places?

ACTIVITIES

a. Use a large sheet of paper. Decorate it by cutting out pictures of the many good things God has given us. In the center of the paper print a simple prayer. Cover it with clear adhesive vinyl or have it laminated. Use this as a place mat to remind you to spend some moments at mealtime talking to your heavenly Father.

b. Use a paper plate and make a simple clock outline. Attach hands with a brass brad so they can be moved. On the clock put "Time to Pray." As a family, talk about the many times each day when you can talk to your heavenly Father.

c. Take turns telling how God answered one of your prayers.

MATERIALS
large sheets of paper
clear adhesive vinyl
magazines
markers
paper plates
brass fasteners

A HILLSIDE SERMON

Matthew 5—7

Devotions outside under a tree or songs sung around a campfire are always special. We feel close to God as we worship outside in His beautiful world. Come along with Jesus as He teaches many people about God on a beautiful hillside.

People had been walking along with Jesus. Finally He told them to sit down, and He taught them. He talked to the crowd about many things. He reminded them of ways to live that would make God happy. He told them to be kind to others and peaceful and loving to their enemies. He reminded them that they were to add flavor to the world like salt adds flavor to food. He told them to let their good works shine out so others would praise God. He used flowers and birds to teach them not to worry. He told them to be ready to help people who were in need. After He taught them many things, He reminded them that it was important to do what He had said.

The people were surprised at all of Jesus' teachings. They said that He taught them with real power and understanding.

PRAYER IDEA
Ask God to help you live so that you please Him.

QUESTIONS

1. What are some things Jesus taught about on the hillside?

2. What surprised the people about Jesus' teaching?

ACTIVITIES

a. Cut a colored tissue in half. Fold each piece with accordion folds. Put the two folded pieces together, and secure the center with a pipe cleaner. Pull each layer of tissue up to the center. Make a bouquet of these flowers for your table. They can help you remember not to worry. You might also give them to a friend and share Jesus' love.

b. Go on an outside treasure hunt. Divide your family into two groups. See which group can first find a leaf with three parts, a bird feather, a pickable flower, a rock, something green, and a circle. When both groups are together, talk about what each item might stand for: 3-part-leaf—the Trinity; bird feather—freedom from worry; flower—God's care; rock—God's strength; green—life; a circle—eternity.

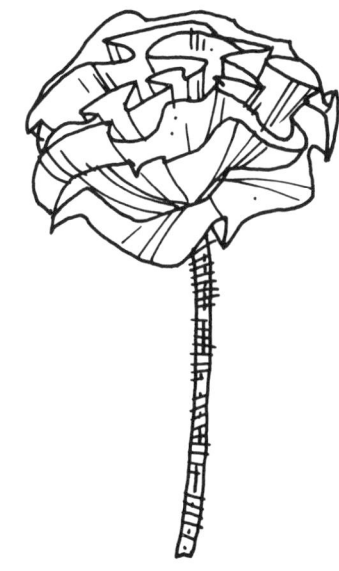

c. Go on a family walk. Use the outdoors as a chance to talk about God's many blessings to your family.

MATERIALS
multicolored tissues   pipe cleaners

TO HEAL A SERVANT

Luke 7:1-10

How do you feel when someone you love is ill? Come along with Jesus as He talks to an army captain who is worried about his sick servant.

First, this captain got some important people to go to Jesus to talk to Him about his servant. These men told Jesus the many kind things the captain had done for them. They told Jesus that he deserved to have his servant healed.

Jesus started for the captain's home. Soon some friends of the captain told Jesus that the captain did not feel he was good enough to have Jesus come to his home. He said that he knew Jesus could heal his servant with a word.

Jesus was pleased at the captain's great faith. He said that He had not found such a great faith in all of His country. When the soldiers got home, they found the servant well. Jesus had healed him.

Jesus can heal our sicknesses. Best of all, He can take away the sickness of sin and make us new people.

PRAYER IDEA
Pray that Jesus will help you always believe in Him.

QUESTIONS
1. Who was ill?
2. Who wanted the sick person healed?
3. Why was Jesus happy with the captain?

ACTIVITIES
a. Take turns telling each other things you believe about Jesus.

b. Make a wordless book. Staple together pieces of dark blue, red, white, green, and gold paper. Use this to tell others what you believe about Jesus. The blue page says I am a sinner. The red page says Jesus died and shed His blood to take my sins away. The white page says now I am cleansed from all my sins. The green page says now I am alive to tell this Good News to others. The gold page reminds us that heaven is our home.

c. Share the story of a person who has told you about his or her faith in Jesus.

MATERIALS
blue, red, white, green, and gold paper

staples or yarn

TO TALK TO JOHN THE BAPTIST'S FOLLOWERS

Matthew 11:1-6

Who is Jesus? Some people say He was a good man. Others say He was a very good teacher. Some say He was a great prophet. Come along with Jesus as some of John the Baptist's followers asked Him just who He is.

John the Baptist was in prison. While he was there, he heard about many things Jesus was doing. He sent his followers to ask Jesus, "Are You the promised Savior, or shall we look for another?"

Jesus told John's followers to tell him about the many things He did. He told them to tell about the blind people, crippled people, and lepers He had healed. He also told them to tell him about the dead people He had brought back to life. In this way Jesus was telling John that He was the Son of God. He was the Savior sent to save the world and give believers in Him life forever in heaven. What a joy to know who Jesus is—our Savior and Lord!

PRAYER IDEA

Pray that the Holy Spirit will give you chances to tell other people who Jesus is.

QUESTIONS
1. What did John's followers ask Jesus?
2. How did Jesus answer their question?
3. How would you tell someone who Jesus is?

ACTIVITIES
a. See how many ways you can finish this sentence: Jesus is... Title it "Jesus is..." Make each page show your idea.

b. Collect and display as many different pictures of Jesus as you can find. What do you think each artist is saying about Jesus from the picture?

c. Make a book by stapling together sheets of paper.

MATERIALS
paper
staples or yarn

pictures of Jesus

TO A STORMY LAKE

Mark 4:35-41

Have you ever been afraid of a storm? Perhaps you heard thunder, saw flashes of lightning, and quickly ran to be close to your parents. Come along with Jesus to a stormy sea.

Jesus had been teaching all day long. He and His followers climbed into a boat to travel on to do more teaching. Soon after the boat left the shore, Jesus fell asleep. The wind blew. The water hit against the little boat. Jesus' followers were afraid. There were sure they were going to drown. But Jesus stayed asleep.

Finally Jesus' followers woke Him up. "Help us, Jesus!" they shouted. "Save us!"

Then Jesus said to the wind and sea, "Be still!" At once everything was quiet. Then Jesus said to His followers, "Why were you afraid? Don't you have faith?"

Jesus' followers were amazed. They said to each other, "Who is this that even the wind and sea listen to Him?'

We who know Jesus as our Lord and Savior have nothing to fear. He is always doing the best things for us.

PRAYER IDEA
Thank God for His control over all weather.

QUESTIONS
1. Where were Jesus and His followers going?
2. What did Jesus do in the boat?
3. Why were the disciples afraid?
4. What did Jesus do?

ACTIVITIES

a. Use crayon and color a picture of a boat on a lake. Use heavy, bright colors. Above the picture print the word "Peace." Make a wash-out of blue or black tempera or water color. Use a lot of water and a little paint. Wash over the boat picture and change the calm scene to a dark stormy scene.

b. Talk about ways God can use storms to bring good to people

c. Staple or tie together sheets of paper to make a simple book. Cut out or draw pictures of things that make people afraid. On the cover print, "Don't be afraid—Jesus is here in..." Look at the pictures and talk about how Jesus helps when we are afraid.

MATERIALS
crayons
tempera or ink
paper
staples or yarn

TO VISIT A SICK GIRL

Mark 5:21-24 and 35-43

Can you think of a time when you (or your brother or sister) were sick? You and your parents were probably eager to do things that would help whoever was ill feel better. Come along with Jesus to visit a sick little girl.

While Jesus was teaching and healing, a ruler name Jairus begged Jesus to come to his house. His little girl was very sick. While Jesus was on his way a messenger came from Jairus's home and said, "Don't bother Jesus anymore. Your little girl is dead."

Then Jesus told Jairus not to be afraid but to believe. He took only Peter, James, and John with him.

When Jesus entered the house, people were crying. Jesus said, "Don't cry; the girl is only sleeping." Then He went into the girl's room and told her to get up. Immediately she got up and walked. Jesus' followers and the girl's parents were surprised.

Jesus had done a miracle and brought the little girl back to life. Jesus still helps people get well and decides when it is time for them to be with Him in heaven.

PRAYER IDEA
Ask God to heal someone who is sick.

QUESTIONS
1. Why did Jairus come to Jesus?
2. What news did the messenger bring?
3. What did Jesus tell Jairus?
4. What miracle did Jesus do?

ACTIVITIES
a. Use a small cardboard box and make a bed. Scraps of material can be the blanket. Use two clothespins, markers, and material scraps to make Jesus and the little girl. Tell the story using this project.

b. In this Bible story Jesus shows He is more powerful than death itself. Think of some ways Jesus shows He is in control over death today (gives people health, heals people doctors think are hopeless).

c. Twist together pipe cleaners to make a daisy. Cut a scrap of material the size of each petal, and glue it under the pipe cleaner. Make a couple of leaves the same way. Get a small cup or flower pot. Put clay or a piece of polystyrene inside to hold the flowers and leaves up. On the container put a small sign: "Jesus cares for you." Give this as a cheer-up to someone you know who is ill or shut-in.

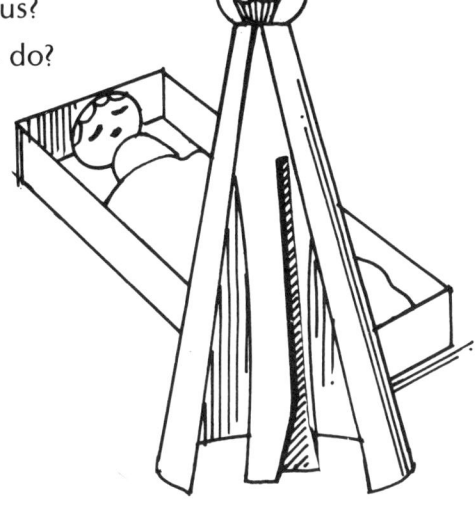

MATERIALS
cardboard box
clothespins
pipecleaners
cup or flower pot
clay or polystyrene
paper or cardboard

TO FEED A HUNGRY CROWD

Mark 6:35-44

"I'm so hungry!" Have you ever said those words? Come along with Jesus as He feeds a hungry crowd.

Jesus was teaching many people in an out-of-the-way place. It began to get late, so His followers said, "Maybe we'd better tell the people to go to a nearby town for supper."

But Jesus said, "You give them something to eat." Jesus' followers wondered if they should go to buy some bread. Then Jesus said, "See how much food we have here." They found that there were five little loaves of bread and two fish.

Then Jesus told the crowd to sit down. He took the food and blessed it. When His followers passed out the food, there was enough for everyone. When everyone was finished eating, there were 12 baskets of food left over. Jesus had done a wonderful miracle to take care of the crowd.

Jesus still takes care of all our needs. Most of all He takes care of our need for forgiveness and a home in heaven.

PRAYER IDEA
Thank God for the food He gives you.

QUESTIONS
1. Why didn't the people have food to eat?
2. What food was there?
3. How were the people fed?

ACTIVITIES

a. Use a cottage-cheese carton. Cover it with brown paper to look like a basket. Cut out five little loaves and two fish from a meat tray, or make them from clay Put them in the basket. Use this as a table centerpiece to remind you that God gives us all our food.

b. Make some simple cookies. Take them to a shut-in or friend and share words about God's loving care for us with them.

c. Cut out pictures of the many kinds of food we have. Over them write, "Lord, bless this food to Your glory and our good." This can be your table prayer for the week.

MATERIALS
cottage-cheese carton
brown paper
meat tray or clay
paper
magazines
glue
crayons or markers
recipe and ingredients for cookies

A STORY ABOUT NEIGHBORS

Luke 10:29-37

Who is your neighbor? Did you name the people who live next door to you? Perhaps you named the people across the street or the people who live in back of you. The neighbor you named might be very close to you or down the road several miles. Come along with Jesus as He tells a story about neighbors.

One day a man had to take a trip. On the way some bad men took his things, beat him, and left him almost dead by the side of the road. A temple priest saw him and walked right by him. So did a man who worked in the temple. Then along came a stranger. He was not even from the same country as the hurt man. This man felt sorry for the beaten man. He took care of his hurts. He put him on his own donkey and took him to an inn for a night's rest. The next day he left money with the innkeeper to care for the man until he was able to go on his way. He even said that if the innkeeper needed more money, he would pay it.

Then Jesus asked this question: "Who was the man's neighbor?" Of course, the people knew it was the man who helped him. We also can be neighbors to people far and near by helping them with the things they need. Who is your neighbor?

PRAYER IDEA

Ask Jesus to help you see what others need and be their neighbor.

QUESTIONS

1. Who did not help the hurt man?
2. Who helped him?
3. What does it mean to be someone's neighbor?

ACTIVITIES

a. Talk about people who have been good neighbors to you. What was your need? How did these people help you?

b. Think about the people who live around you. What are some of the things they need? (Ideas: a visit if they are lonely, help in their yard, someone to run an errand, etc.) Do a "good neighbor" project for them.

c. Use old magazines or newspapers. Cut out pictures of people who are being good neighbors. Make these pages into a scrapbook. Give them to your church nursery, a sick friend, or a nursing home or hospital.

MATERIALS

old magazines
paper
glue
scissors
cardboard or heavy paper for book covers
yarn or ribbon to lace pages together

A MEETING ON THE WATER

Matthew 14:22-33

Did you ever see a friend far away or in a dim light and not recognize who it was? Come along to the sea and a time when Jesus' followers did not recognize Him.

Jesus was busy saying good-bye to the crowds. He sent His followers ahead of Him in a boat. After everyone was gone, Jesus spent some time alone praying. Finally He began to walk across the water to meet His followers. When they saw Him coming, they thought He was a ghost.

Jesus said, "Don't be afraid."

Then Jesus' friend Peter said, "Jesus, if it is You, tell me to come to You on the water."

Jesus said, "Come."

Then Peter began to walk to Jesus, but when he saw the wind and waves, he became afraid and began to sink. Jesus caught him and asked, "Why did you doubt?" Then Jesus and Peter got into the boat. All Jesus' followers said that Jesus was really the Son of God.

We too can tell each other who Jesus is. We can know He is our Savior from sin and our best friend.

PRAYER IDEA
Ask Jesus to help you to trust Him when you are afraid.

QUESTIONS
1. Why were Jesus' followers afraid?
2. What did Jesus say to His followers?
3. Who wanted to walk to Jesus?
4. Why did he begin to sink?
5. Who did the followers say Jesus was?

ACTIVITIES
a. Write or tell about a time you were afraid. How does it help to know Jesus is always with you?

b. Cut out or draw pictures of times, places, or things that may cause people to be afraid. Over the pictures write Jesus' words "Have no fear."

c. Use a walnut shell half or a plastic cap. Put a bit of clay into it and insert a paper sail on a toothpick. This little boat can remind you not to be afraid.

MATERIALS
paper
crayons, paints, or markers
walnut shell or plastic cap
clay
toothpick

TO A FRIEND'S FOR SUPPER

Luke 10:38-42

Come over for supper. It's fun to visit friends and share a meal. It's fun to share the joy of Jesus with others. Come along with Jesus to visit His friends Mary and Martha.

When Jesus got to His friends' home, Martha invited Him in. She was busy hurrying to prepare a meal for Jesus. Mary sat at Jesus' feet. She was busy listening to the many things Jesus was teaching about God. Soon Martha became angry because her sister was not helping. She said to Jesus, "Don't You care that I have to do all the serving alone? Tell Mary to help me."

But Jesus said, "Don't worry about so many things. One thing is the most important—to hear God's Word. Mary has picked the important thing."

We can be busy in the best way when we spend some of our time hearing and learning God's Word. It is the most important thing for us to do in this life.

PRAYER IDEA
Ask the Holy Spirit to keep you excited about studying God's Word.

QUESTIONS
1. Whom was Jesus visiting?
2. What was Martha doing?
3. What was Mary doing?
4. Which sister picked the most important thing to do at that time?

ACTIVITIES
a. Take turns listening to and sharing God's Word by telling your favorite Bible section or story.

b. Cut a ribbon or paper into a bookmark shape. Cut out the letters of the word JOY. Use this bookmark in your Bible or devotional book to remind you to keep Jesus and His Word first, Others second, and Yourself last.

c. What would you do if (1) your friend invites you to go roller-skating—on Sunday morning during your church time? (2) you have time for family devotions if you miss your favorite television program? (3) during church your friend keeps whispering to you?

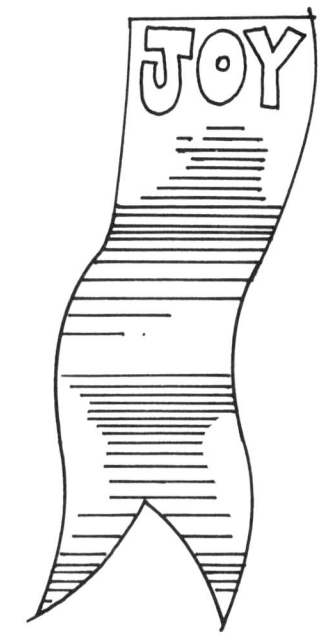

MATERIALS
ribbon
paper
felt
glue

A MEAL AT SIMON'S HOUSE

Matthew 26:6-13

Let's go along with Jesus to Simon's house. Simon had once been sick with leprosy. Jesus had made him well. Now Simon wanted to be kind to Jesus and thank Him by inviting Him to his house for a meal. While Jesus was there, a woman came up to Him and poured some sweet-smelling perfume that cost a lot of money on Jesus' head. Jesus' followers scolded her because they thought this woman had wasted her money on the perfume. They thought the money could have been spent better if she had given it to help poor people.

Jesus told His followers that they should leave the woman alone. He said that she had done a very special, kind thing for Him. He also said that wherever people heard the Good News that He was the Savior from sin, they would also hear what a loving thing this woman had done.

Think of the wonderful things Jesus has done for you. What kind of things can you do for others that will show them that you love Jesus?

PRAYER IDEA

Ask Jesus to give you chances to tell your friends about His love.

QUESTIONS

1. Why do you think the woman brought the perfume gift to Jesus?
2. How did the disciples feel about her gift?
3. How did Jesus feel about her gift?
4. How can we give gifts to Jesus today?

ACTIVITIES

a. Have an older family member put some strongly scented items in small containers. Put them in several look-alike brown paper bags. Turn turns sniffing the scents. See if family members can guess the item by the scent. Suggestions: cloves, cinnamon, mint, lemon, onion.

b. Make a list labled "SWEET SMELLING GIFTS." As family or class members, put on the list any sweet, kind deeds you see others doing for Jesus.

c. Make a pomander ball using cloves and an orange, or make scented sachets. The pomander ball is made by pressing whole cloves in tight touching rows over an entire orange. Sachets could be made by putting dried flowers or scented cotton into small squares of material. Give these items as love gifts to a shut-in friend or neighbor. Perhaps their sweet scent will give you a chance to tell of the sweetness of Jesus' love.

MATERIALS

strongly scented items such as
    cloves, cinnamon, mint, lemon, and onion
an orange
whole cloves
dried flowers
material scraps
yarn
scented cotton balls

TO HELP A POOR WIDOW

Luke 7:11-17

Have you ever seen someone crying and, although you really did not know him, you wanted to do something to help him? Come along as Jesus helps a poor widow.

Jesus was just outside the city of Nain. He saw a crowd of people. A woman was crying. Jesus learned that her husband had died, and now the body of her only son was being carried out to be buried. How lonely and sad the woman felt!

Jesus looked at her and felt sorry for her. He said to her, "Don't cry." Then He touched the cot on which the body was being carried, and the people who were carrying it stopped.

Jesus said to the body, "Young man, I say to you, arise." The young man sat up and began to talk.

How happy this mother must have been! The people around said, "A great prophet is with us. God has visited His people." Soon this news spread everywhere.

Jesus still has power over death. Believing in Him gives us life forever in heaven.

PRAYER IDEA
Thank Jesus for His power over death.

QUESTIONS
1. Why was the mother sad?
2. How did Jesus feel?
3. What did Jesus do?

ACTIVITIES
a. Make a card for someone who is ill or lonely. Be sure to remind him that Jesus cares for him.

b. Finish this sentence: "I am glad to know Jesus has power over death because..."

c. Name as many times as you can from God's Word when someone came back to life.

MATERIALS
paper
fabric scraps
glue
markers or crayons

AN EYE-OPENING EXPERIENCE

John 9:1-38

Sometimes we say the light goes on. Other times we say our eyes are opened. What we mean is that we understand something that we did not understand before. Come along with Jesus as He gives a young man an eye-opening experience.

Jesus was walking along when He saw a man who had been blind since he was born. Jesus said that He needed to do the work of God who sent Him. He also reminded His followers that He was the Light of the world. He spat on the ground and made some clay. He put the clay on the man's eyes and told him to go wash in the pool of Siloam.

After the blind man did this, his eyes were opened. He could see clearly. Then the man also had his eyes opened to the truth. Jesus was a prophet. He also knew that He was a man sent from God. He told Jesus that he believed in Him.

All who know Jesus as their Savior and Lord have seen clearly. They know that Jesus forgives sins and gives them a heavenly home.

PRAYER IDEA

Pray that many will have their eyes opened to the truth about Jesus.

QUESTIONS
1. What was the trouble with the man in the story?
2. What did Jesus do for him?
3. What was the most important eye-opener in the story?

ACTIVITIES
a. Use clay to make a model of the blind man.

b. Use your eyes to read a story to a younger or older friend who would enjoy your company. If you can't read, you can tell your favorite story.

c. Put items such as sandpaper, fur, an apple, a paper clip, a ball, a pencil, etc., in a bag. Can you identify them by how they feel? Think about what a great blessing your sight is.

MATERIALS
clay
sandpaper
fur
apple
paper clip
ball
pencil
bag

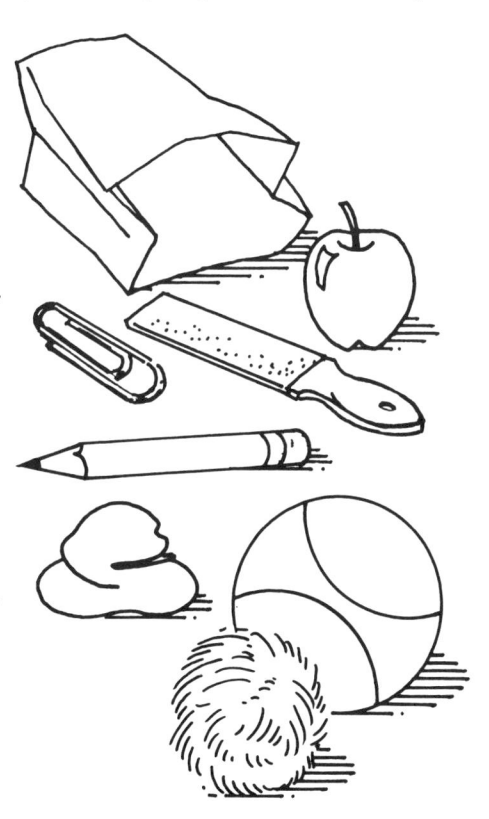

TO HEAL 10 MEN

Luke 17:11-19

Think of a time when you got something you wanted very much. Maybe it was a toy you had waited for or a special game. How did you feel? What did you say? Come along with Jesus as He gave 10 men something they wanted very much.

Jesus had just come to a little town when He was met by 10 men who were sick with leprosy. People who had this sickness had to stay away from all other people because others might get the sickness from them. These sick men called to Jesus and begged Him to make them better. Jesus told them to show themselves to the priests. This was what they needed to do to be sure they were better and could go back and live with their families and friends again.

The 10 men went on their way. One looked down and saw that his sickness was gone. He ran back to tell Jesus thank you. Jesus said, "Didn't I heal 10 men? Where are the other nine?" Only one man came back to say thanks.

Have you remembered to thank Jesus for all the wonderful things He has done for you?

PRAYER IDEA

Thank Jesus for times He has made you better when you were sick.

QUESTIONS
1. What did the 10 men want?
2. What did Jesus do for them?
3. What did the men do after they found out they were better?

ACTIVITIES
a. Write a thank-you note or draw a thank-you picture for someone who has done a "loving Jesus" thing for you.

b. Cut out pictures and make a collage of the many things for which your family can say thank You to Jesus.

c. Make a list of sick people for whom your family can pray. Thank Jesus, too, when they are well again.

MATERIALS
paper
crayons or markers
magazines
glue

TO SIT ON JESUS' LAP

Mark 10:13-16

It is always a good feeling to climb on the lap of someone you like or to get a hug or a kiss from a favorite relative or friend. It is wonderful to know someone cares about you. Come along with Jesus as He holds and blesses some children.

Jesus was busy teaching. Some mothers came and brought their children for Him to touch and bless. But Jesus' followers felt the mothers should not bother Jesus. They thought He was too busy and had more important things to do. They told them to go away. When Jesus heard this, He was unhappy. He said, "Let the children come to Me. My kingdom is made up of people who simply believe like a child." Then Jesus picked up the children, put His hands on their heads, and gave them God's blessings.

How wonderful to know that we too can always go to Jesus for His love and blessing! He cares for us so much.

PRAYER IDEA
Thank Jesus that you can come to Him.

QUESTIONS
1. Who was coming to Jesus?
2. Why were they coming?
3. What did Jesus' followers tell them?
4. What did Jesus say to the women and children?

ACTIVITIES
a. Talk about times when people, especially children, get a blessing today (Baptism, confirmation, Communion, etc.).

b. Find as many pictures as you can of Jesus and the children. How do you think Jesus felt about children? Why?

c. Fold sheets of paper four times. Draw some simple paper dolls. Have the arms on the fold and do not cut them. On these simple paper dolls letter "Jesus loves children." Talk about how Jesus shows His love for children.

MATERIALS
paper
crayons, pencils, or markers

TO A PLACE ABOVE A CITY

Luke 19:41-44; 13:34

Remember a time when you looked at your parents and saw that they were unhappy about something you had done. Maybe you saw hurt or tears in their eyes. You knew that you had let them down. Come along with Jesus as He cries over the city of Jerusalem.

Jesus is looking at Jerusalem and thinking about the people from His own country. He has tried so often to help them understand that He is their Lord and their promised Savior. He had said that He would like to keep His people close to Him like a mother hen keeps her baby chicks close so that they will be safe from any danger. He wants them to know His love and to care for Him. But His own people will not listen to Him. How sad Jesus was that they did not know the joy and peace of having Him as their Savior. It is wonderful today when people turn to Jesus and know Him as their friend and Savior. What a blessing to be close to Jesus!

PRAYER IDEA
Pray for someone who does not know Jesus or needs to be closer to Him?

QUESTIONS
1. Why is Jesus sad?
2. What does Jesus want His people to know about Him?

ACTIVITIES
a. Draw a picture of a mother hen. Use cotton puffs and color them yellow with powdered tempera or yellow chalk. Glue on beaks and eyes and color on legs below the puff. Put these little chicks snuggled close to the large hen. Use this picture to remind you how close we can be to Jesus.

b. Cut out pictures that show people doing bad things. Let it remind you that many people do not know Jesus or His love. This picture can also remind you to pray for people who do not yet know Jesus.

c. Talk about a time when you felt especially close to Jesus.

MATERIALS
cotton puffs
yellow tempera powder or chalk
magazines or newspapers
paper
glue
crayons or markers

TO VISIT SAD FRIENDS

John 11:1-44

What do you do or say when someone you love dies? Come along with Jesus as He visits friends whose brother died.

While Jesus was teaching, news came to Him that His friend Lazarus was ill. After a two-day wait, Jesus and his followers went to Lazarus's village. Soon they heard that Lazarus was dead. Martha heard that Jesus was there and ran to meet Him. She told Jesus that she knew He could have made Lazarus well and that even now He had power over life and death because He was the Son of God.

Martha called Mary. Mary came and fell at Jesus feet crying. Jesus cried too. Then He asked Mary to take Him to the tomb. When they got there, Jesus asked them to take the stone away. Then Jesus prayed and thanked God for hearing His prayer. He said that what was going to happen would help people believe. Then He said, "Lazarus, come out." At once Lazarus came out of the grave. Jesus had brought His friend back to life. He still gives all His friends who believe in Him life forever.

PRAYER IDEA
Thank Jesus for His power over death.

QUESTIONS
1. Who had died?
2. How did Martha and Mary feel about their brother's death?
3. What did Jesus do? Why?

ACTIVITIES
a. The circle is a symbol of eternity (life forever). Use lightweight cardboard. Cut out a large circle. Then cut out seven smaller circles. Color the circles bright colors. Attach them to the large circle and create a mobile. This mobile can remind you of the life forever you have with Jesus.

b. Read together the book, *If I Should Live, If I Should Die*, by Joanne Marxhausen (Concordia Publishing House).

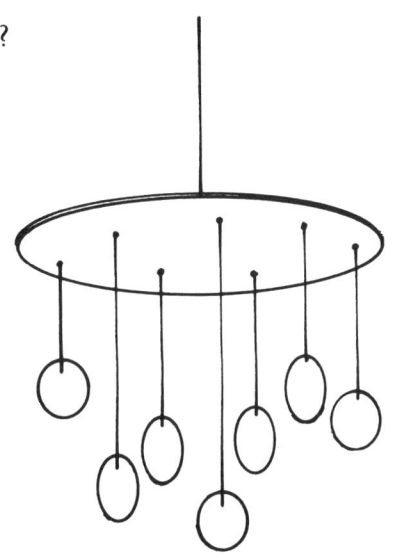

c. What are some things you might say or do for someone who is feeling bad that someone they love has died?

MATERIALS
lightweight cardboard
scissors

crayons or markers

TO A POOLSIDE

John 5:1-9

Did you ever need just a little help to get something you wanted? Perhaps you needed someone to lift you up to reach your light switch or a toy off your high shelf. Maybe you needed a little help in getting dressed or combing your hair. Come along with Jesus to a pool where He gave a man all the help he needed.

Jesus had come to visit a special pool. At certain times God would give this pool the power to make the first person who got in it well. As Jesus came to the pool, He spoke to a crippled man who had been waiting by the pool for 38 years. Jesus asked him, "Do you want to be well?"

The man answered, "Yes, but when the water has its power to heal, I have no one to take me down and put me in it."

Jesus knew that He could help the man. He said, "Get up, take your bed, and walk."

At once the man was better. Now he could walk. Jesus had given him the help he needed. Jesus also gives us the help we need. He gets rid of our sin so we can call heaven our home.

PRAYER IDEA

Thank Jesus for helping you with the things you need.

QUESTIONS
1. Why was this pool special?
2. Why had the man waited so long by the pool?
3. What do you think the man thought about Jesus after He had healed him?

ACTIVITIES
a. Say a special prayer of thanks for a time when Jesus helped you.

b. Draw a picture or mural of today's Bible lesson.

c. Make a finger or paper-bag puppet to be the crippled man. Let the puppet tell the story of what Jesus did for him.

MATERIALS
paper
crayons or markers
a paper bag

TO A FIG TREE

Matthew 21:18-22

Did you ever save a cookie or a piece of candy for a snack later on and when you went back to get your treat, it was gone? Someone had already enjoyed your snack. How unhappy and disappointed you felt! Come along with Jesus as He, too, faces disappointment.

As Jesus is walking with His disciples, He feels hungry. He sees a fig tree by the road and looks on it for a snack. Some fresh figs would taste so good. What disappointment! The fig tree has only leaves. There are no figs. There is no snack for Jesus. Then Jesus says that no figs will ever come on that tree because it did not grow any fruit.

Jesus often calls the kind things we do because we love Him our good fruits. When we are close to Jesus, the good things we do come naturally. What special things have you done because you love Jesus? Does Jesus look at you and see good fruits?

PRAYER IDEA
Pray that God will help you have many good fruits in your life.

QUESTIONS
1. What did Jesus expect to see on the fig tree?
2. What fruit does Jesus expect to see from us?

ACTIVITIES

a. Work together and cut up fresh fruits for a special fruit salad. Let everyone have a part washing, peeling, or cutting. Talk about the fruits of Christian living like love, joy, peace, patience, etc.

b. Cut out the shapes of a variety of fruits. Color each fruit and write on it a good deed fruit of love you have seen in your family. Tie your fruits to a hanger to make a simple mobile.

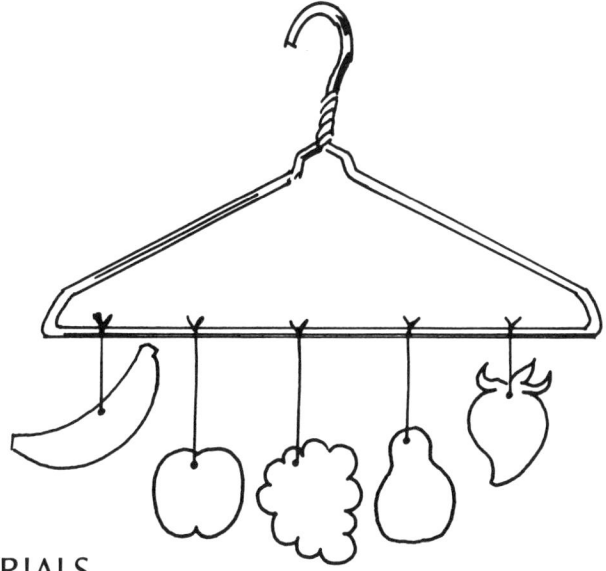

MATERIALS
knives
various fruits for fruit salad
clay
paper or lightweight
   cardboard
crayons or markers
hanger
thread or string

TO VISIT A TREE CLIMBER

Luke 19:1-10

Tree climbing is always fun. Each branch puts you up a bit higher. It's fun to see the world from such a high place. Come along as Jesus visits a tree climber.

Jesus was walking through Jericho. There were many people around Him. A rich man named Zacchaeus was very short. Among all the crowds of people he could not even get a peek at Jesus. Then he had an idea. He ran ahead and quickly climbed into a tree waiting for Jesus to pass by.

When Jesus came to the place where Zacchaeus was perched, He stopped and looked up. How happy and surprised Zacchaeus was when Jesus said, "Come down, Zacchaeus. Today I am coming to your house to stay." Zacchaeus had thought Jesus would not be interested in someone who had done bad things like he had done. But Jesus showed Zacchaeus that no one is too bad or too small for Him to love.

PRAYER IDEA

Ask Jesus to help you love all people as He does.

QUESTIONS
1. Why couldn't Zacchaeus see Jesus?
2. How did he solve his problem?
3. Why was Zacchaeus surprised that Jesus stopped and talked to him?

ACTIVITIES
a. Find a small branch. Anchor it with clay into a jar lid. Make a drawing of little Zacchaeus. Cut it out. Glue it to a clamp-type clothespin, and clip Zacchaeus into your tree branch. Use this to tell the story and to help you remember that Jesus loves all people.

b. Set an extra place at your table today. Pray and ask Jesus to be your special guest. Talk about what it means to have Jesus as a visitor. Remember that Jesus is always visiting with you.

MATERIALS
branch
clay
paper
clamp clothespin
crayons or markers

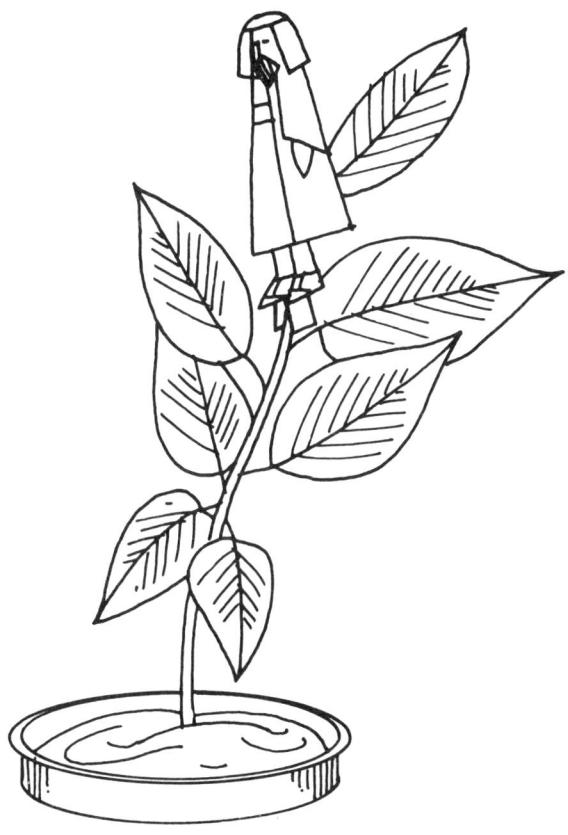

TO JESUS' HOME
Luke 4:16-30

When heroes or stars return to their hometowns, they are greeted one of two ways. Sometimes people are proud of someone who has come from their town. They put up signs to say, "Look who comes from our town." Other times heroes are overlooked in their homes. People say, "Oh, it's just John. I remember when he was a boy. He can't be too important." Come along as Jesus returns to His home.

Jesus went to His home church. There He was asked to read from the book of Isaiah. He read about someone who was sent to preach good news to the poor, release captives, and give sight to the blind. Then He told them that this part of God's Word was talking about Him.

The people were surprised at His words. They said to each other, "Isn't this the son of Joseph the carpenter?" Finally, as He spoke more to them, they became angry. They were even going to throw Him head first down a hill, but He left them.

People who knew Jesus so well had trouble accepting Him as their Messiah and Savior.

PRAYER IDEA
Ask Jesus always to stay with you in your home.

QUESTIONS
1. What did Jesus tell the people about Himself?
2. Why did the people have trouble believing this?

ACTIVITIES
a. Write a newspaper article or draw a news picture about Jesus' return to His home.

b. Draw a picture of your house. Cut out a picture of Jesus from a bulletin or Sunday school lesson. Glue this picture to your house to remind you to welcome Jesus to your home.

MATERIALS
paper
crayons or markers
glue
pictures of Jesus

A TALK WITH A RICH YOUNG MAN

Mark 10:17-22

What is your favorite thing? What do you have that you love the most? What would you hate to lose the most? Come along as Jesus talks to a young man whose favorite thing was money and what it could buy.

One day a young man came to Jesus. He asked Jesus what he should do to have life forever in heaven. Jesus said that he should keep all the commandments. The young man said that he had done this since he was young.

Jesus loved the young man. He knew that this young man loved things more than God, so He gave him a command to help him think. He said, "Sell everything you own, and give the money to the poor." At this the young man left. He was not willing to give everything up for Jesus. He could not say that loving God was more important to him.

What is the most important thing in your life?

PRAYER IDEA

Ask God to help you keep loving Him as the most important thing in your life.

QUESTIONS
1. What questions did the young man ask Jesus?
2. How did Jesus answer him?
3. What was most important to this young man?
4. What was keeping this young man from heaven?

ACTIVITIES
a. Cut two pieces of felt like the paper pattern. Sew them together on the dotted line. Punch holes on the dots. Put a ribbon or heavy yarn through to draw the pouch together. Use this pouch for your money for Jesus. Talk about the ways we can use our money to make Jesus happy.

b. Cut out pictures of things which people may love more than Jesus. Talk about ways to put God first in your life.

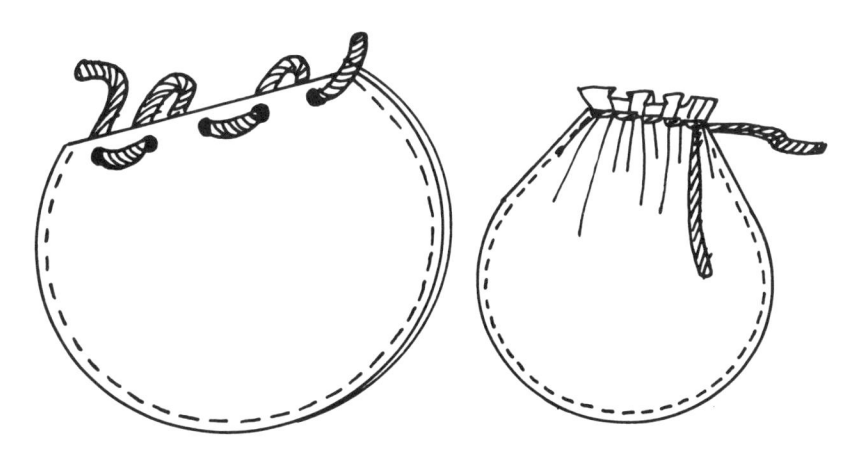

MATERIALS
felt
thread
yarn
hole punch
scissors
catalogs or magazines

A POOR WOMAN'S OFFERING

Mark 12:41-44

It's always fun to give something to Jesus. Sometimes we give our money. Sometimes we give our songs and praise. Sometimes we find ways to do good and kind things for others. These show Jesus that we love Him. Come along with Jesus as He watches a poor woman give her offering gift.

Jesus was at the temple church with His followers. He was watching people put money into the temple offering box. Some rich people put in a lot of money. Some poor people put in very little money. Finally a poor woman came by and put in two coins worth about a penny. When He saw this, Jesus said, "She has given more than anyone. The other people gave a little bit out of all they had. This woman gave everything she had."

We, too, can give gifts of love to make Jesus happy. We can find ways to follow Jesus' will and make our lives a gift to our wonderful Savior.

PRAYER IDEA
Ask Jesus to make you a joyful giver.

QUESTIONS
1. Where was Jesus and His followers?
2. Why was Jesus happy with the woman's gift?
3. When do our gifts make Jesus happy?

ACTIVITIES
a. Wrap an empty box to look like a present. Put a slot in the top. As a family, use this to collect change for several weeks. At the end of this time give your money to some project like a missionary, world hunger, etc.

b. As a part of this devotion sing several of your favorite songs as gifts to Jesus.

c. When we do kind things for others, it is like we are doing them for Jesus. Make five coupons of jobs you will do for different people as a gift to Jesus.

MATERIALS
empty box
wrapping paper and tape
paper
crayons or markers

TO OPEN EARS

Mark 7:31-37

Did your mom or dad ever say to you, "Open your ears!"? They did not think there was a problem with your hearing. They were telling you to use your ears well to listen to what they had to say to you. Come along with Jesus as He meets a man who cannot hear or speak.

As Jesus was walking along, people brought this man to Him. He took him off where they could be along. Then He put His fingers in the man's ears and touched the man's tongue with His finger. Then He said, "Be opened."

All at once the man could hear. He could also speak clearly. The people standing around were surprised. They said, "Look! Jesus does everything well. He can make deaf people hear and He can make people who are unable to talk speak very clearly."

Jesus still opens people's ears. He helps them to hear and understand God's Word more clearly. He also helps them speak about the wonderful things He has done for them. People today are still surprised by the many wonderful things Jesus has done for them.

PRAYER IDEA

Ask Jesus to keep your ears open to His Word and your mouth ready to speak about Him.

QUESTIONS
1. What problem did the man in the story have?
2. How did Jesus show He cared about the man?
3. How does Jesus open ears and mouths today?

ACTIVITIES
a. Make a list of all the things you can find that Jesus did well while He lived on this earth.

THINGS JESUS DID
1. CURED THE SICK
2. FED THE HUNGRY
3. HELPED THE POOR
4. TAUGHT PEOPLE RIGHT FROM WRONG
5. TAUGHT DISCIPLES

b. Pray this action prayer:

Open my ears to hear Your Word. *(Point to ears.)*
Open my mind to understand. *(Point to head.)*
Open my heart to know Your love. *(Point to heart.)*
Open my mouth to speak about You. *(Point to mouth.)*

c. Make a collage of ears and mouths. Put this lettering on it: "Open my ears to hear. Open my mouth to speak."

MATERIALS
paper
old magazines
glue
crayons or markers
scissors

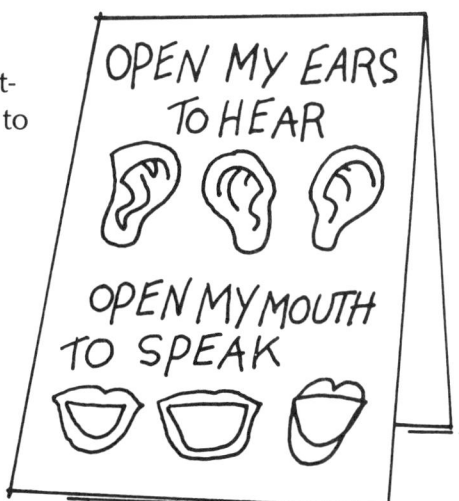

A LESSON ON PRAYER

Luke 11:1-4

You may have listened to your parents answer the telephone many times. One day you decide that you, too, would like to learn to answer the phone. You ask your parents just what is the best way to answer the phone. Then your parents give you a lesson on what to say.

Jesus' disciples had often heard Him talk with His heavenly Father. They saw the help and strength He got from these talks. Come along as they ask Jesus to teach them to pray.

Jesus gave His disciples a sample prayer. We often call it the Lord's Prayer. In this prayer Jesus tells His followers to call God Father and to talk to Him as they would to a loving Father. He tells them to praise God, to ask Him for things they need for life on earth and things to keep them close to Him. He reminds them that it is important for them to ask God to do what is best for them. He tells them they can ask God to forgive all their sins.

PRAYER IDEA
Put the words of the Lord's Prayer into your own words.

QUESTIONS
1. What did Jesus' disciples want to learn?
2. What prayer did Jesus teach them?
3. What are some parts of the Lord's Prayer?

ACTIVITIES

a. Read the Arch Book on the Lord's Prayer to help you understand this special prayer.

b. If you do not know it, work together to learn to say the Lord's Prayer. Say it with your devotions this week.

c. Make a picture to go with each part of the Lord's Prayer. Hang it near where you pray to remind you of the parts of this prayer.

d. Have each person in your family make up some special prayers. Write them down and put them together in a special family prayer book. You might want to give this booklet to a special friend or relative.

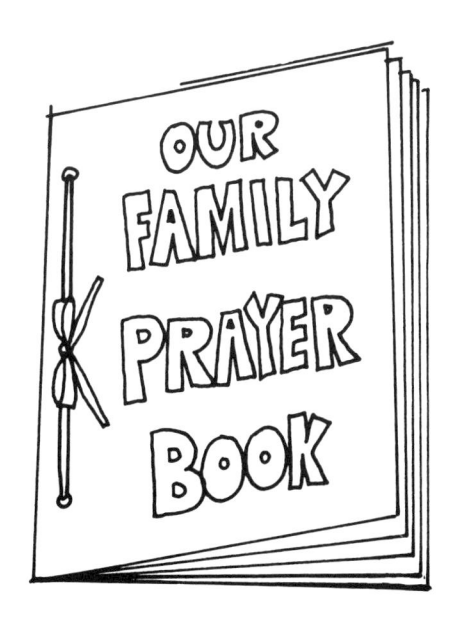

MATERIALS
Arch Book of the Lord's Prayer
paper
crayons or markers

A MOUNTAIN VISION

Mark 9:2-9

Wow! What a great vacation! We had so much fun and saw so many beautiful things that I wish we never had to go home. Did you ever feel this way? Come along with Jesus as He shares a wonderful scene with Peter, James, and John.

One day Jesus took Peter, James, and John up on a mountain. While they were there, Jesus was changed in a special way. His clothes were shiny and white. Then Elijah and Moses also appeared. Peter was excited. What he saw and felt was so wonderful that he asked Jesus if he could make little huts and they could just stay there.

A voice from heaven told everyone that Jesus was God's Son and they should listen to Him. Then Elijah and Moses were gone. Jesus knew He had a job to do; He was to die and save the world. He told His followers that they must leave the mountainside.

Although we don't see special visions, we can see many wonderful things about Jesus in God's world. Then we need to get on with our work of doing what God's Word tell us and sharing that Word with others.

PRAYER IDEA
Thank God for times you feel especially close to Him.

QUESTIONS
1. Where did Jesus take Peter, James, and John?
2. What did they see there?
3. Why did they leave the mountain?

ACTIVITIES
a. Look over old vacation pictures. Talk about times when your family has been especially close to each other and to God.

b. Take turns choosing and singing favorite Jesus songs. Pick ones that make you feel excited and happy that Jesus is your Savior.

c. Do the following finger play:

> Climb on a mountain, *(Make fingers climb an invisible mountain.)*
> A wonderful sight. *(Put hands over eyes.)*
> Jesus' clothes are shiny white. *(Point to your clothes.)*
> A special voice to make it clear: *(Point to your throat.)*
> Jesus is God's Son so dear. *(Put arms to chest in hugging action.)*
>
> (Original - J. Groth)

MATERIALS
old vacation pictures

SENDING OUT THE DISCIPLES

Matthew 9:35—10:16

Many Boy and Girl Scouts learn what to do on a camp-out. They practice setting up tents, building fires, and cooking. Finally the time comes when they go out on their first real camp-out. They put into use all the things they have learned about camping.

Jesus had taught His followers. He had shown they in many ways that He was the promised Savior. He had shown them His power. He had shown them that He was God.

One day Jesus called His followers together. He sent them out two by two. He told them not to take money or extra clothes along with them. They were to go to many villages of the people of Israel. They were to tell that Jesus, the promised Messiah, the Son of God, had come. They were to do all the things Jesus told them. Jesus gave them power over unclean spirits and every disease.

Jesus has sent all Christians out also. Christians are people who follow Jesus. He has given them His Word as the power to change people's lives. Jesus wants all who love Him to share the Good News that He is the Savior.

PRAYER IDEA

Ask Jesus to send out many people to share His Good News with others.

QUESTIONS

1. How has Jesus helped His followers get ready for their job?
2. What power did Jesus give His followers?
3. What job do Jesus' followers have today?

ACTIVITIES

a. Write a letter or draw a picture for your pastor. Thank him for sharing the Good News of Jesus with you.

b. Hang up a world map. Pray each day for people in a different country who do not know Jesus.

c. Sing "This Little Gospel Light of Mine." As you sing it, ask Jesus to make you shine with the Good News He has given you.

MATERIALS

paper
crayons or markers
a world map

A LOOK AT THE FUTURE
Mark 8:31-33

Do you ever wonder what the future will bring? Perhaps you wonder whom you will marry, what you will do when you grow up, or where you will live. Come along with Jesus as He tells His disciples about His future.

Jesus was busy teaching His followers. He told them that He would suffer many things. He told them that the church leaders would not believe that He was the Son of God. He also told His followers that He would be killed. Then He gave them the good news that after three days He would rise again.

One of Jesus' followers, Peter, could hardly stand for Jesus to talk about these things. Peter did not want these bad things to happen to Jesus. But Jesus said that it was really the devil trying to get Him to forget the job He had come to do here on earth.

How wonderful that Jesus was ready to suffer and die for the sins of man! It is good to know that He died and came back to life for us.

PRAYER IDEA
Dear Jesus, thank You for being with us to face the future.

QUESTIONS

1. Why do you think Jesus told His followers what was going to happen to Him?

2. What was Jesus' job on earth?

ACTIVITIES

a. Cut out pictures to make a booklet of what you would like to do with your future.

b. Use paper bags or large sheets of paper to make hats for a variety of occupations. Thank God for the many jobs that give everyone a chance to serve Him.

MATERIALS

paper bags
crayons or markers
glue
large sheets of paper
magazines

IN A PARADE

Matthew 21:1-11

The sounds of the band come to our ears. The clowns pass by. Floats go by with pretty girls or children throwing candy. The fire engines blow their sirens. There is clapping and cheering. A parade is always a happy and exciting event.

Come along with Jesus on a very special parade. As He rides along the path, people think of how wonderful He is, who He is, and the many great miracles He has done for them. They shout happily, "Hosanna to the Son of David! Blessed is He who comes in the name of the Lord! Hosanna in the highest!" There are loud shouts by children and parents telling everyone how wonderful Jesus is. Some people cut down palm branches. Some people lay their coats down to make a soft path for Jesus to ride over. It is a happy crowd that greets Jesus, the promised Messiah. We too can shout for joy that Jesus is our King.

PRAYER IDEA
Thank Jesus for something special He has done for you.

QUESTIONS
1. Why are the people happy?
2. What do the people do to show that they love Jesus?
3. What are some ways you can tell Jesus today how wonderful He is?

ACTIVITIES
a. Decorate wagons and bikes and make posters. Have a happy parade to share the joy of Jesus with your neighborhood. You might hand out balloons that are lettered with markers and say, "Jesus Loves You."

b. Cut a palm branch from paper. Color it green. Letter it with the words "Hosanna to Jesus." Hang it up to remind you of Jesus' coming for you.

MATERIALS
paper
crepe paper
tape
scissors
markers or crayons
balloons

TO A SPECIAL SUPPER

Luke 22:14-23

Come along with Jesus to a special supper. Jesus is spending some time with His followers before He suffers and dies. They are sitting around the table talking. Jesus says a prayer. Then He takes the bread and wine from supper. He takes the bread and says, "This is My body." He takes the wine and says, "This is My blood." Then He passes the bread and wine to His friends. He tells them that whenever they have this special meal, they will remember Him.

Today people who have the bread and wine of this special meal and hear God's Word about it call it the Lord's Supper. As they eat it, they remember Jesus' suffering, dying, and rising for them. They know that through this meal God will strengthen their faith in Him, forgive their sins, and help them to face sadness, hurt, and troubles in their daily lives. Jesus' meal for His followers that night is a wonderful blessing for His followers of today, too.

PRAYER IDEA

Ask Jesus to help you remember Him as you work and play each day.

QUESTIONS
1. What food did Jesus use in the Lord's Supper?

2. Why do you think Jesus gave this special meal to His disciples that night?

3. Why do Christians receive the Lord's Supper today?

ACTIVITIES
a. Make some unleavened bread like Jesus used in the Lord's Supper and taste it. Here is the recipe:

3 cups whole wheat flour
1 1/3 — 1 3/8 cups of water

Mix the ingredients together but do not overknead. Cover a cookie sheet with brown paper and sprinkle with extra flour. Spread the dough to the edges like pizza. Score deeply (but not completely through the dough) into ½-inch squares. Bake in a 375 degree oven for 15 minutes on each side (use no grease). Use brown paper to turn the bread. Remove the paper, and bake the last 15 minutes. Dust off excess flour. Cool and turn over several times. When the bread is cool, place it on a tray with a terry cloth towel. The bread can be baked the night before tasting.

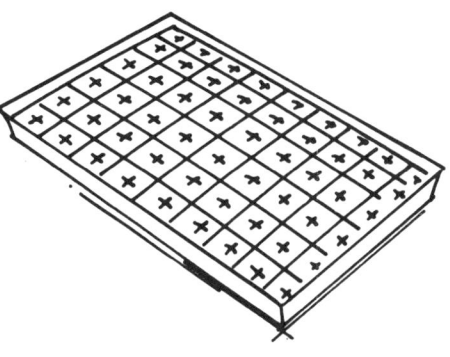

b. Take a look at the communionware at your church. What symbols or pieces help you remember the first Lord's Supper? Why?

MATERIALS
whole wheat flour
water
bowl
brown paper
cookie sheet

TO A FOOT WASHING

John 13:1-20

There are some jobs that most people do not like to do. A common job for people in Jesus' day was to wash people's feet. Paths were dusty, and most people wore sandals, so foot washing was a kind thing to do for a visitor to your home. Come along with Jesus to a foot washing.

Jesus was getting ready for a special meal with His followers. After the disciples sat down, Jesus got up, laid aside His robe, and got a towel. After He poured water in a bowl, He began to wash His disciples' feet.

Peter was upset when Jesus came to him. He did not feel that Jesus, his Master, should be bending down to wash his dusty feet. But Jesus said that He must wash Peter's feet so that Peter could be a part of Him.

Then Jesus told the disciples why He had washed their feet like a servant. He told them that to be great in God's sight you must be willing to do simple jobs and kind deeds for others.

In our lives we can ask the Holy Spirit to make us ready to serve others and help them in their needs.

PRAYER IDEA

Ask God to make you ready to serve those around you so that they will see that Jesus lives in you.

QUESTIONS

1. What did Jesus do for His followers?
2. Why didn't Peter want Jesus to wash his feet?
3. What was Jesus teaching His followers?

ACTIVITIES

a. Find a way to do some kind of service for each person in your family this week. Perhaps it could be a job that is not so exciting, like hanging up clothes, cleaning shoes, etc. Think about Jesus' lesson to His followers as you do this job.

b. On a paper towel print the words of Jesus, "Do as I have done to you." Use this towel to help you do a job for someone. (Older children might embroider these words on a plain cotton towel.)

MATERIALS

paper towels
crayons or markers
cloth towel
various colored embroidery flosses
needles

TO A GARDEN TO PRAY

Mark 14:32-42

At times all of us have known something that we should do. Maybe we wished we did not have to do it. Perhaps it was our job, but we thought that if we waited long enough, we would not have to do it, or we would find a more pleasant way to do it. Come along with Jesus to the Garden of Gethsemane as He prays about His job.

When Jesus and His followers reached the Garden of Gethsemane, Jesus went off by Himself to pray. He talked to His heavenly Father and asked that, if it was His will, He would take away His painful job of suffering and dying. Then He told God that He should do whatever was the best. Next He went to talk with His followers, but they were sleeping.

Three times Jesus went by Himself to pray to His heavenly Father to ask Him for another way to save the world if it was possible. He always asked that God's will be done. When He finished praying, an angel came to give Him strength to do the hard job of suffering and dying for our sins.

PRAYER IDEA
Ask God to help you to do His will.

QUESTIONS
1. For what did Jesus pray?
2. What did Jesus come to do on earth?

ACTIVITIES
a. God always plans what is best for us. Add Jesus' words to your prayers: "Thy will be done."

b. Find a flat stone. On it paint a cross and the words "Your will be done." Use it to help you remember that God's plan is always best for our life.

c. Kneel to say your prayers this week. This will help you remember that you are bending to what God has planned for you.

MATERIALS
flat stones
acrylic paints

A GARDEN MEETING

Mark 14:43-46

There are many ways of showing that we love someone. Sometimes we do it with a smile, a pat, a hug, or a kiss. Come along as one of Jesus' followers uses a kiss as a signal to His enemies rather than a sign of love.

When Jesus had finished praying to His heavenly Father, a crowd of men suddenly came into the Garden of Gethsemane with swords and clubs. Then Judas, one of Jesus' followers, came up to Jesus. He had given the men a sign that the person he kissed was Jesus. Then they would know whom to tie up and take away.

When Judas saw Jesus, he said, "Master!" and kissed Him. Then the men grabbed Jesus. Judas had turned Jesus over to wicked men. He had not been a true, loving friend of Jesus. Jesus lovingly and willingly went to suffer and die for the sins of all people. He took these hurts on Himself to make us friends of God.

PRAYER IDEA

Ask God to keep your lips true to your love for Jesus.

QUESTIONS
1. Who turned Jesus over to the evil men?
2. What sign showed the men who Jesus was?
3. Why did Jesus let the men take Him away?

ACTIVITIES
a. Visit a person in your community (a neighbor, a shut-in, or someone in the nursing home). Show them some true Christian love with a hug or a friendly smile.

b. Cut out lips from a magazine. Make a collage with them. Talk about ways our lips can be used to please Jesus. Talk about ways our lips can be used to make Jesus unhappy. Title your collage "Lips for Jesus' Love."

MATERIALS
magazines
paper
glue
crayons or markers

TO A HIGH PRIEST'S COURT

Mark 14:53-65

Sometimes people are cruel and tell lies or say that someone did something that they did not really do. If you have had this happen to you, you will know how terrible it makes you feel. Come along with Jesus as He stands before a church court.

The people in the court do not believe that Jesus is the promised Savior. They are looking for people to tell lies about Jesus. But even the people who are telling lies cannot agree on their lies. Finally, the head of the group asks Jesus if He is the Son of God. When Jesus says yes, he becomes very angry and says that Jesus is speaking against God.

Although Jesus was telling the truth, this group says He deserves to die. Then they spit on Him and hit Him. Jesus willingly takes all this.

Jesus suffered all these lies and took all this unfairness and hate for us. He took shame and hurt that we deserve so that He could take our sins away. What a loving Savior we have!

PRAYER IDEA
Ask Jesus to forgive your sins.

QUESTIONS
1. What did people tell about Jesus?
2. Who did Jesus say He was?
3. What did the court say should happen to Jesus?
4. Why did Jesus let people lie about Him and hurt Him?

ACTIVITIES
a. Sing "Jesus Loves Me."

b. Talk about bad things we do each day to make Jesus unhappy. Ask Jesus to forgive these sins. Think of ways you can stop doing some particular sin. Ask Jesus to help you.

c. Jesus said that He was the Son of God. Cut a big sun out of yellow tissue paper. On it letter, "Let the Son shine in." Hang it in your window to remind you to let God's Son, Jesus, shine in your life.

MATERIALS
yellow tissue paper
markers or crayons

AT A FIRESIDE
Luke 22:54-62

Has anyone ever made fun of you for going to Sunday school or church? Sometimes it is hard to stand up and say you are a Christian. Come along with Jesus as He looks and reminds a follower that he is one of His friends.

While the church leaders were talking to Jesus, Peter was sitting outside by a fire keeping warm. A young girl saw him and said, "Aren't you one of Jesus' followers?"

Now Peter was afraid and he said, "I don't even know him."

Then another person said, "This man is one of Jesus' followers."

But Peter said, "Oh no! You're wrong!"

Still another person said, "This man was with Jesus."

But Peter said, "I don't even know what you're saying."

Then a rooster crowed, and as Jesus was being led away, He looked at Peter. Suddenly Peter remembered what Jesus had said. Before a rooster crowed in the morning, he would say three times that he was not one of Jesus' friends. Peter went out and cried over his sin. We can be glad that Jesus is ready to forgive us when we do not act like we are His followers.

PRAYER IDEA

Ask God to help you stand up for Jesus and be one of His good followers.

QUESTIONS

1. What did Peter say when people said that he was a follower of Jesus?
2. Why did Peter answer this way?
3. What made Peter think about his sin?

ACTIVITIES

a. Draw an outline of a rooster on cardboard. Fill in this rooster shape by gluing on different types of seeds and grains or different shapes of macaroni and spaghetti. After the glue is dry, cover it with a clear sealer. Hang the rooster someplace in your home to remind you that Jesus is ready to forgive your sins the way He forgave Peter.

b. Talk about this question: If someone came into your home, how would they know that your family follows Jesus?

c. Make a sign for your bedroom: "One of Jesus' friends lives here." Decorate it.

MATERIALS

cardboard
scissors
seeds or pasta
clear sealer
paper or cardboard
crayons or markers

TO ANOTHER TRIAL

Mark 15:1-15

Many people today try to forget there is a God. They want to live in their sinful ways and forget that there is a good and right way to live. Come along with Jesus as the crowd shouts that they want to get rid of Him.

The church leaders could not put anyone to death so they sent Jesus to the Roman ruler Pilate. When Jesus got to Pilate's court, Pilate asked Him, "Are you the King of the Jews?"

Jesus answered, "You have said it correctly." Jesus was telling Pilate that He had come to be the promised Messiah. Then the church leaders said many bad things about Jesus. Jesus did not answer them. He said nothing to defend Himself. Pilate was surprised that Jesus kept quiet. He tried to find a way to free Jesus but the crowd kept shouting, "Kill Him!" Finally he gave in to the people and said, "All right, go and kill Him by hanging Him on a cross."

The people had not made Jesus their Lord and King.

PRAYER IDEA
Ask Jesus to be the real king of your heart and life.

QUESTIONS
1. Who did Pilate say Jesus was?
2. Was he correct?
3. What did the crowd want to do to Jesus?

ACTIVITIES
a. Make a paper crown. Talk about what kind of a king Jesus is.

b. Sing one verse of "The King of Glory Comes" (*Joyful Sounds* [Concordia Publishing House], page 40).

MATERIALS
paper and crayons
scissors

THE SOLDIERS' MEAN GAME

Mark 15:16-20

It is no fun to have people make fun of you. It makes us feel hurt and unhappy. Come along with Jesus as some soldiers make fun of Him.

Pilate had said Jesus could be killed. Now the soldiers led Him away. They remembered that someone had said He was a king, so they decided to have some mean fun. They found an old purple coat. They put it on Jesus for a king's robe. They took some thorns and made a crown to push on His head. They made fun of Jesus and said, "Hail, King of Jews!" They hit Jesus on the head with a stick and spit on Him.

Jesus did not have to put up with this. He took all these hurts willingly. It was part of the hurt He chose to put up with to pay the price of our sins. He suffered for us because He loves us so very much. He bore all these hurts so that our sins would be forgiven. He gave His life so that we could enjoy life forever with Him in heaven.

PRAYER IDEA
Thank Jesus for suffering for you.

QUESTIONS
1. What did the soldiers do to Jesus?
2. Why did Jesus put up with this meanness?

ACTIVITIES
a. Find or draw a picture of today's Bible story. How does this picture make you feel? Why? Thank Jesus for all He has done for you.

b. The soldiers called Jesus "King of the Jews." What are some names you call Jesus because you love Him?

MATERIALS
paper
crayons
pictures of the mockery of Jesus

ON A HARD WALK

Luke 23:26-31

Have you ever gone on a hard walk? Maybe the ground was rough or rocky. Perhaps the path was uphill, or there were many weeds and bushes in the way. Come along with Jesus on a hard walk.

The path Jesus is walking on is clear. The road is not hard to follow, but it is hard for Jesus to walk along this way. He knows what is at the end of the road. He is walking along carrying His heavy cross. He has had a hard night, and He is very tired. All our sins are resting on Him. He is on His way to suffer and die for all the bad things we and all people have done. Jesus' walk is not easy.

While He is walking along, Jesus stumbles. The soldiers grab another man to help Him carry His cross. The people along the way are crying for Him, but Jesus tells them not to cry for Him. He tells them that they should be sad for themselves if they do not come to know Him as their Savior. Jesus walked this hard way for us. He walked all the way to the cross so that when our life here is over, we can go all the way to heaven with Him.

PRAYER IDEA

Thank Jesus for walking all the way to the cross for you.

QUESTIONS
1. Why was Jesus' walk a hard one?
2. Why did Jesus walk the way to the cross?
3. Whom did Jesus say the people should cry for?

ACTIVITIES
a. Take a hike in your favorite park or down your favorite path. As you are walking, think of Jesus' walk for you.

b. Trace around your feet on heavy cardboard, and cut out the shapes to make sandals. Use yarn to make sandal tie-ons. On them write, "He walked for me."

c. Run an errand for your mother, father, or a shut-in friend or neighbor. Let your steps of love remind you of Jesus' walk of love for you.

MATERIALS
cardboard crayons or markers
yarn scissors

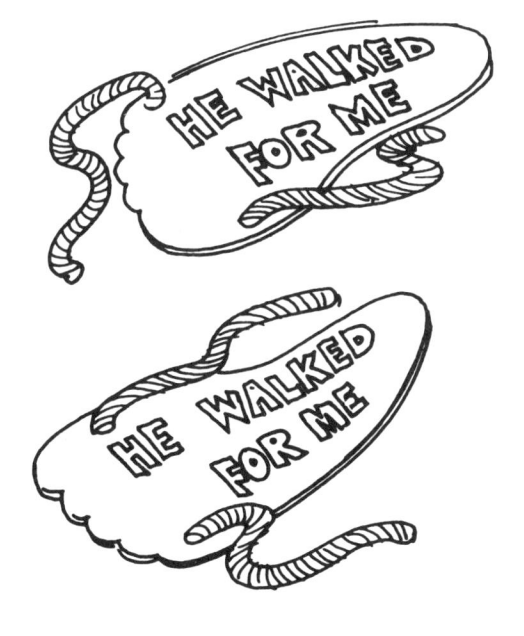

AT THE CROSS
Luke 23:32-43

Sometimes when we are sick or busy, we do not think of others. We think about what is hurting us or what we have to do. Jesus always thought about and cared for others. Come along and see Jesus as He hangs on the cross.

Jesus' enemies had done their worst. They had made Him suffer. Now He was hanging on the cross and was going to die. Hanging beside Him were two bad men. They deserved the hurt they were getting, but Jesus had done nothing wrong. Even now Jesus showed His great love for others. When the one bad man asked Jesus to remember Him when He came into His kingdom, Jesus showed He forgave the man for the bad things he had done by promising that he would be in heaven with Him that very day. Jesus also told one of His friends to care for His mother, Mary. Jesus cared for others to the very end. His greatest loving and caring was His death itself. By this He gave life forever in heaven to all who know and love Him as their Savior.

PRAYER IDEA
Ask Jesus to help you show His care and love to others.

QUESTIONS
1. Who was dying with Jesus?
2. How was Jesus different from the two men?
3. How did Jesus show that even while He was on the cross, He cared for others?

ACTIVITIES
a. Cut a cross out of heavy paper or lightweight cardboard. Make slits every half inch but do not cut through the edge. Weave a strip of ribbon or pretty paper in and out through the slits. Give this cross to someone you love and care for. It might be a good chance to share Jesus' love with them, too.

b. Sing "There Is a Green Hill Far Away" (*Joyful Sounds* [Concordia Publishing House], page 38).

c. Make up a litany. Have each person say a loving thing Jesus has given to them. Let everyone respond with, "Thank You, Lord Jesus, for loving and caring for us."

MATERIALS
heavy paper
strips of paper or ribbon

TO SEE JESUS DIE

Luke 23:44-49 and John 19:28-30

Have you ever worked long and hard at making something or at a job like cleaning your room? When you were all done and looked at your work, you may have said, "Wow! Am I glad that's done!" Come along with Jesus as He finishes His work here on earth.

Jesus has been hanging on the cross. Some people around Him are crying. Others are making fun of Him. Some soldiers are playing a game to see who will win Jesus' clothes. Finally a great darkness covers the earth. Jesus is about to die. He talks to His heavenly Father and says, "Father, I put myself into Your hands." Then He says, "It is finished," and dies.

Jesus' work is done. He has lived a perfect life. He has suffered and died. He has done everything needed to save all people. His death gives life to all who believe in Him as their Lord and Savior.

PRAYER IDEA
Ask Jesus to help you always to remember that He has done everything needed to save you.

QUESTIONS
1. What things are happening around Jesus as He hangs on the cross?
2. What does Jesus mean when He says, "It is finished"?

ACTIVITIES
a. Using a shoe box, paper, material, sticks, etc., make a diorama of today's story.

b. Make a sign saying "It is finished" for a cross in your house, or make a cross out of cardboard or wood. Use it to remind you that Jesus has done everything you need to go to heaven.

c. Use some of your time today to finish a project or job that you have begun.

MATERIALS
shoe box
paper
sticks
stones

material
cardboard
glue
crayons or markers

TO THE TOMB OF JESUS

Luke 23:50-56

Death is a part of our life. Maybe a pet of yours has died. Perhaps someone in your family or a friend's family has died. It makes us feel sad when someone we care about dies. We miss them. Come and see as Jesus' friends take care of His body.

Jesus had died. A friend of Jesus named Joseph asked for Jesus' body. Then he took the body down from the cross, wrapped it in linen cloths, and put it in his own new rock tomb. Some women who were friends of Jesus saw His body put into the tomb. They hurried home to prepare spices and oils to put on His body.

No doubt all of Jesus' friends were feeling sad that their great Teacher and Friend was dead, and they would never see Him again. Perhaps they felt the worst as they thought that Jesus was not the promised Savior for whom they had waited.

But we look at that tomb and feel both sad and happy. We are sad that Jesus had to suffer and die for our sins, but we are also happy that He not only died but also came back to life for us. For us the tomb says, "Jesus is the winner."

PRAYER IDEA

Ask Jesus to remind you that death for a Christian is the way to life forever.

QUESTIONS
1. What happened to Jesus?
2. What did Joseph do with Jesus' body?
3. How did Jesus' friends feel?

ACTIVITIES
a. Make a model of the tomb out of clay. (It must have looked something like a cave.) On it put a sign: "He died for me."

b. Read the book *If I Should Live, If I Should Die* by Joanne Marxhausen (Concordia Publishing House).

c. Plant some seeds in a carton or pot. Although the seeds look dead, soon they will grow new live plants. How is this like today's Bible story?

MATERIALS
toothpicks or sticks
paper
carton or pot
seeds
dirt

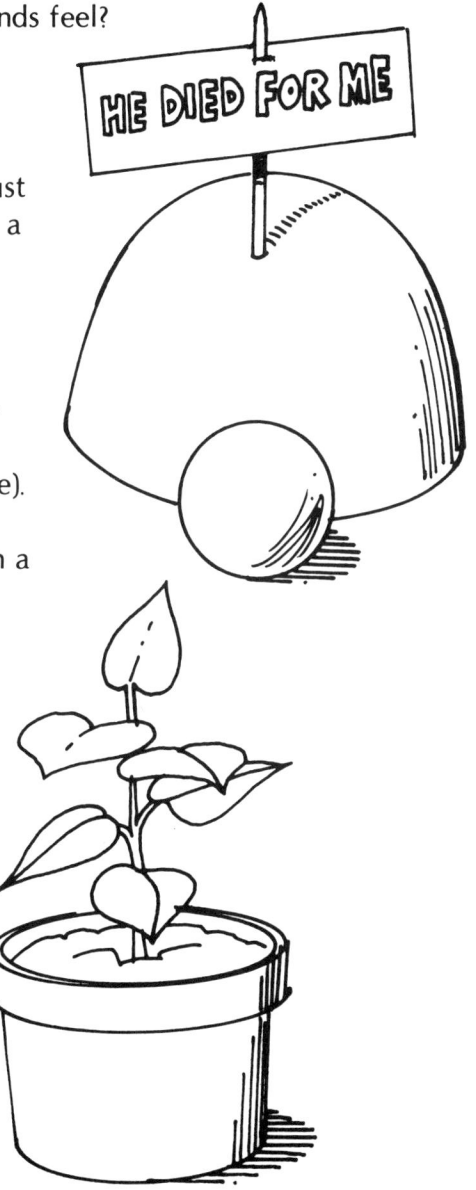

IN THE TOMB'S GARDEN
John 20:1-18

Have you ever walked through a cemetery? Many people are buried there. Come along to the garden of the tomb where Jesus' body was placed.

Mary Magdalene had gone to the garden where Jesus' tomb was. When she arrived, she saw that the stone that had been rolled against the opening was gone. Immediately she was afraid and upset. She ran to get Peter and John.

These two friends ran back together to the tomb. They saw the clothes which had been around Jesus' body were now rolled up and laid aside. Then wondering, afraid, and confused, Peter and John ran back home.

Mary, however, took a closer look into the tomb. There she saw two angels who asked her why she was crying. She answered that she was sad because Jesus' body had been stolen. When she turned around, she saw a man who she thought was the gardener. She heard a voice call, "Mary." At once she knew it was Jesus. She ran to tell Jesus' friends the good news.

Jesus was alive! He had won the fight over death.

PRAYER IDEA
Thank Jesus for His Easter victory and the home He has won for you in heaven.

QUESTIONS
1. Why was Mary upset that the stone was taken away from the tomb?
2. What did Peter and John see at the tomb?
3. Whom did Mary see at the tomb?
4. What did Mary now know about Jesus?

ACTIVITIES

a. A lamb is one of the pictures of Jesus as the winner. Make a lamb cake or a plain cake and letter it THE WINNER. As you share the cake, let it remind you of the sweetness and joy of Jesus' victory for you.

b. Decorate hard-boiled eggs first with wax or crayons saying "He lives" or "The Winner." Then dye the eggs. The egg stands for new life. Remember Jesus' new life for you.

c. Cut out the outline of a butterfly. Cut one-inch squares of brightly colored crepe paper. Stretch them over the eraser end of a pencil. Put a dab of glue on this and attach it to the butterfly outline. Keep the crepe-paper cups close together and cover the entire butterfly. This butterfly is a symbol of new life. When we look at the cocoon, we see no life. Then the butterfly comes out and shows a beautiful new life.

MATERIALS
cake mix and frosting
crayons
egg coloring or food coloring
cardboard
crepe paper in various colors
glue
eggs

ON THE EMMAUS ROAD

Luke 25: 13-34

Sometimes taking a walk helps us think. Come along with Jesus' followers as they take a walk.

While two of Jesus' friends are walking and talking, Jesus came and began to walk and talk with them. But they did not realize it was Jesus. As they walked, they talked about their friend Jesus. They talked about how sad and disappointed they were that He had died. Then they talked about the news they had heard that He was alive again.

Soon Jesus began to explain many things to them. He told them how the Bible promised that the Savior would suffer and die. He also reminded them that it said He would come back to life.

When they got to their village, they begged their fellow walker to stay with them. He did. Then they sat down to eat a meal. When the traveler took bread and prayed, they knew at once that it was Jesus. Then Jesus disappeared.

Immediately they ran to tell the others. They wanted to share the news that Jesus was really alive.

PRAYER IDEA
Ask Jesus to help you share the Good News of Easter with someone who does not know it.

QUESTIONS
1. What did the men talk about as they walked?
2. What things did Jesus tell them?
3. When did they realize who Jesus was?
4. What did they do then?

ACTIVITIES
a. Make an Easter card. Write the words, "Jesus died and came back to life for you." Send it to someone with whom you would like to share the Good News of Easter.

b. Make an Easter play to share with your friends or family. You might act out this Bible story.

c. Make a brightly colored banner or flag for your door or window. On it write the words "Jesus Lives!" You might decorate it with Easter lilies or a butterfly.

MATERIALS
paper
materials for banner
glue

IN A CLOSED ROOM
John 20:24-30

Sometimes we feel that something is too good to be true. We may feel this way when our parents buy something that we have been wanting for a long time. Thomas must have felt this way. He said, "I want to see the nail scars in His hands. I want to see the spear mark in His side. Then I will believe." Come along as Jesus appears to Thomas and to some of His other followers.

The followers of Jesus were meeting together. Suddenly Jesus was right in the middle of their group. He said, "Peace be to you." Then he spoke to Thomas and told him to go ahead and touch the nail and spear marks so he could really believe that He was alive.

But Thomas did not need to do this. When he looked at Jesus, he called out at once, "My Lord and my God!" Jesus said it was good that Thomas believed after he had seen Him. He also said that people are blessed who believe without seeing Him in person. Jesus was talking about us. We haven't seen Him, but we believe.

PRAYER IDEA
Thank God for the faith in Jesus that He has given you.

QUESTIONS
1. What did Thomas want to see so that He could believe in Jesus?

2. What did Thomas say when he saw Jesus' hands and side?

3. Who did Jesus say was blessed?

ACTIVITIES
a. Make a collage by cutting out many pairs of eyes. Label it: "We do not see but we believe."

b. Talk about ways we can "see" Jesus without using our eyes (in the actions of others, in His Word, etc.).

MATERIALS
magazines
paper or posterboard
glue
markers or crayons

TO A SEASHORE BREAKFAST

John 21:1-14

Did you ever get up early for a hike? Perhaps as you walked you felt very close to Jesus. You saw the sunrise and the beauties of God's creation. Come along as Jesus prepares an early morning breakfast for His followers.

Jesus' followers had worked all night fishing. As day was breaking, Jesus stood on the beach. He called out and asked them if they had caught any fish. They said no. Then Jesus told them to cast the net on the right side of the boat and they would find some. Immediately their nets filled with fish. John knew at once that it was Jesus. He told Peter that it was their Lord.

Peter jumped into the water and swam to shore. When the others came in by boat, Jesus told Peter to bring some of the fish. Then Jesus fixed breakfast. When He gave them fish and bread, there was no doubt in their minds. It was their wonderful risen Lord. As we read God's Word, Jesus shows Himself to us. We also know that He is our Lord and Savior.

PRAYER IDEA
Thank Jesus that you know Him as your Savior.

QUESTIONS
1. What miracle did Jesus do?
2. When did the disciples know for sure that it was Jesus?

ACTIVITIES
a. Take an early morning hike. Name as many things as you can that remind you of your wonderful God.

b. Use a sand table or sandbox, a toy boat, a piece of net, and clothespin people to retell today's Bible story.

MATERIALS
sand table or sandbox
toy boat
net
clothespins
crayons or markers
material scraps

TO A HILLSIDE GATHERING

Matthew 28:16-20 and Luke 24:50-53

Many times Jesus had taken His disciples off to a hillside to teach and talk with them. At these times He had taught them things they would need to know when He was gone. Come along with Jesus as He takes His disciples to another hillside scene.

Jesus and His followers went to a hillside after He rose from the dead. There Jesus talked to His disciples. He told them that He had all power in heaven and earth. Then He gave all His followers some directions about their job. He told them to share the Good News that He had died and come back to life with all people. He wanted people everywhere to become His followers. Then He reminded them that He would always be with them.

Another time, after Jesus spoke with His followers, He raised His hands and blessed them. Then He went back to heaven. The disciples stood a few minutes. Then they realized that they had better get busy with their task.

Jesus' words are important to us, too. They remind us of our job to share the Good News with all people.

PRAYER IDEA
Pray that you will have a chance today to share the Good News of Jesus with someone.

QUESTIONS
1. Where did Jesus take His followers?
2. What were Jesus' last words?
3. Where did Jesus go?

ACTIVITIES
a. As a family, write a letter or send a treat package to a missionary. Thank him for sharing the Good News of Jesus with people in another part of the world.

b. Take turns telling each other what you believe about Jesus. Pictures or blue, red, white, green, and gold paper may help you. (Remember the wordless book we made, page 41?)

c. Hang a world map near your devotion area. Take turns praying for people in different countries who do not know Jesus. Pray that someone will speak the Good News to them.